THE SECRET TEACHINGS OF
AIKIDO

THE SECRET TEACHINGS OF
AIKIDO

MORIHEI UESHIBA

PREFACE BY
MORITERU UESHIBA

TRANSLATED BY
JOHN STEVENS

KODANSHA USA

CAPTIONS

TITLE PAGE: Morihei Ueshiba painted as a Dragon King.

ABOVE: *Agatsu / Morihei*
"Self-Victory, [signed] Morihei."

Contact information for the Aikikai Foundation:

Aikido World Headquarters
Aikikai Foundation
17–18 Wakamatsu-cho,
Shinjuku-ku, Tokyo 162–0056   Japan
Tel: 81–(0)3–3203–9236
Fax: 81–(0)3–3204–8145
Website: www.aikikai.or.jp
E-mail: aikido@aikikai.or.jp

Edited in cooperation with Musashi Editorial Ltd., and Matt Cotterill.

Published by Kodansha USA, Inc.
451 Park Avenue South, New York, NY 10016

Distributed in the United Kingdom and continental Europe
by Kodansha Europe Ltd.

First edition published in Japan in 2007 by Kodansha International
First US edition 2012 by Kodansha USA

19 18 17 16 15 14 13 12   8 7 6 5 4 3 2 1

The Library of the Congress has cataloged the earlier printing as follows:

Library of Congress Cataloging-in-Publication Data

Ueshiba, Morihei, 1883-1969.
   The secret teachings of Aikido / Morihei Ueshiba ; preface by Moriteru Ueshiba ;
translated by John Stevens.
      p. cm.
   ISBN 978-4-7700-3030-6
   1. Aikido. I. Title.
   GV1114.35.U46 2007
   796.815'4--dc22
                                              2007036406

CONTENTS

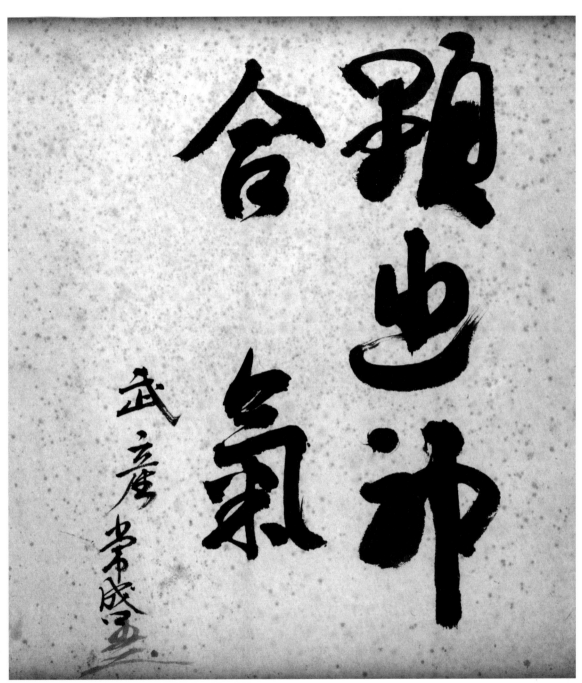

Ken Yū Shin / Aiki / Takemusu Tsunemori
"Manifest, Hidden, Divine: Aiki, [signed] Takemusu Tsunemori."

PREFACE

Aikido is a modern *budo* founded by Morihei Ueshiba based on his training in the traditional martial arts of Japan and his rigorous spiritual practices. Morihei developed his art into a Way over fifty years ago, and it was through the tireless efforts of his son and successor Kisshomaru Ueshiba that the philosophy and techniques of Aikido became known all over the globe. In a mere half-century, Aikido—what the Founder called the "Spirit of Harmony"—is now practiced by people in some ninety different countries. Aikido has spread everywhere.

Although the practice of Aikido has become widespread, however, misunderstandings and misinterpretations of the philosophy of the art have occurred. It is our responsibility to present the true spirit of Aikido, not just its physical aspects, in order to further, and correctly advance, the cause of Aikido in contemporary society.

This present book is a translation of a collection of the Founder's lectures, edited by the second Doshu Kisshomaru. They were first published in the *Aiki Shimbun*. The Founder's talks present the inner teachings of Aikido, so this book is not at all a technical manual. It describes the core of the Founder's spirit and his interpretation of the techniques.

I will be very happy if those who are engaged in heartfelt Aikido training make this book of the Founder's lessons their daily companion and study his words often. This was also the sincere hope of the Founder and the second Doshu Kisshomaru, who are surely pleased by the publication of this international edition of *The Secret Teachings of Aikido*.

Moriteru Ueshiba
AIKIDO DOSHU

Ame no murakumo kuki samuhara ryu-o / Bushin / Morihei
"*Ame no murakumo kuki samuhara ryu-o, Divine Bu,* [signed] Morihei."

I

AIKIDO IS
THE STUDY OF
THE SPIRIT

Aikido is the study of the spirit. Aikido is the subtle breath linking the spiritual and material, the *A* [alpha] and *UN* [omega] of existence. Aikido is additionally the sacred manifestation of the functioning of the universe; it is the supreme law that reveals the active principles underlying the nature of things, and the manner in which the world operates. All things originate from one source; each spiritual and material element emerges from that single source. That is the subtle manner in which life functions. These principles give birth to existence; they bind spirit and matter. This is how life unfolds in the grand scheme of things. The universe is all like one family, and the subtle breath of life envelops past, present, and future; comprehending that principle will help guide us in all aspects of our lives. Since the universe originates and develops from one source, we should always optimistically seek unity and harmony in all our endeavors.

We must rely on the battle cry *Masakatsu agatsu katsuhayabi* [True victory is self-victory, a victory right here, right now]. That spirit enables us to become one with the universe and its operation and allows us to develop the inner and outer realms of existence—such knowledge reverberates throughout the whole body, removing all obstacles and purifying our faculties. Realize that the source of the universe and the source of your own life are the same, and do not underestimate the power of the

Morihei with André Nocquet, one of the early foreign students of Aikido.

concept of *Masakatsu agatsu katsuhayabi*. Rely on the supreme power of *takemusu no bu no a-un* [valorous, creative living from start to finish] to create spiritual techniques and walk along the Way.

That is the meaning of *aiki* [harmonious energy]. Use the sword to truly harmonize your breath and extinguish all evil. The purpose of Aikido is to elevate ourselves from the world of matter to the world of the spirit. Matter descends, the spirit ascends. Aikido is a wonderful flower that blooms in our world and bears great spiritual fruit. Aikido should be the basis of our lives, and we should strive to establish true goodness, true love, and true sincerity everywhere.

Those who earnestly desire to make progress in Aikido must always keep these principles in mind; perceive the universe as it really is, root all your actions there, and open your own individual gate to the truth.

At present, this is the age of materialism. We must strive, however, to make the flower of the spirit bloom and to bear spiritual fruit. In that manner, the spiritual element will become more pronounced. If it does not, this world will never improve. Materially and scientifically the world has advanced greatly, but it will be infinitely better if more spiritual fruit is nourished. Try to make this happen every single day.

In my heart, I always attempt to stay centered between heaven and earth and in tune with the universe. When I face an important challenge, beams of white light appear before me and I can stand boldly, without fear, amid any turmoil. Because I am free of trivial self-conceit, if an opponent thrusts with a fan, I can read his movements and use my own fan to counter-thrust. This is not a trick but a matter of hard training. Train like this, and you will be sure to make progress.

Regarding the movements of the body, they are just like the movements of waves—when a wave peaks, when an attack comes, it becomes yang, and reverberates. An inhalation is not simply a pulling in of air but a dynamic act of filling your entire being with subtle breath. An exhalation is to expel the energy of the divine source. In the realm of everyday life in the world, gather up your own universal breath and purify society with divine energy.

Since the intention of an attack is triggered by a beam of light, focus your spirit there. Use your own light to neutralize it, to become one with it. Employ that light as a bridge, a place where you can advance, and try to experience this each day.

Life gives us four great treasures: (1) the energy of sun and moon; (2) the subtle breath of heaven; (3) the subtle breath of earth; and (4) the rising and falling of the tide. These four great treasures we must thoroughly comprehend.

One more treasure—a pure and radiant jewel of a mind—is also necessary. These five treasures will allow us to purify the world and harmonize all hostility. It is not just Ueshiba who can do this—anyone who agrees

Morihei demonstrating a sword take-away technique.

with these ideas will receive a guiding light from heaven and feel a powerful inspiration. We need people who will bloom and bear spiritual fruit, people who will guard the three worlds of Hidden, Manifest, and Divine.

Build a *stupa* [Buddha tower] within yourself. We need more than just buildings of wood or stone, we need an inner construction of the spirit. I long for that day to come. Then people will be able to transform themselves into Kanzeon Bodhisattva [female Bodhisattva of compassion] or Saisho Nyorai [male Buddha of supreme victory] in order to save all sentient beings. The country of Japan will then become like one huge Buddha *stupa*. To actualize such a state, to bring it closer into being, is the reason for practicing Aikido.

Material culture has advanced, resulting in the creation of such objects as television, a machine that enables us to see images thousands of miles away. We must advance beyond reliance on such mere contraptions and make the flower of the spirit bloom and bear fruit; then each person will be on the same wavelength and be able to read one another's mind like a picture.

In Aikido, before an opponent can take a solid stance before us, we must absorb his spirit completely. Use the gravity of your spiritual power to advance. It is possible to perceive the entire world in a single glance. However, no one today, including myself, can accomplish this feat.

Religious people often talk about "calming the spirit and returning to the source" (*chinkon-kishin*) but many do not really seem to understand the concept. One can become shackled by one's own egoism, and this is bad. Find your true self and then you can nourish your body and spirit. Do not neglect this.

When we consider the material world, we see that the six sense organs [eyes, ears, nose, tongue, skin, consciousness] must be cleansed in order to make progress. If there is no clarity, confusion results. If the senses are clogged, disorder and evil appear in the world. Creating disturbance in this world is the worst sin. Cleanse your heart and liberate your senses, then you can act freely without obstructions, and the spiritual path will become clear. Your sense organs will radiate with light. But it is not just the sense organs that must be purified—the entire world needs to be cleansed and chaos dispelled.

Aikido follows the truth of the universe and reveals the inner principles of existence. However, as I often say, each person must understand this in his or her own way. Those who are practicing in an enlightened manner base their movements on the "one-sword single body" principle [in other words, "no duplicity"]. They never stop refining their character. This Way cannot be expressed in words or theories but must be found in the resonance (*hibiki*) that sustains existence. The Way is like the flow of blood within one's body. One must not be separated from the divine mind in the slightest in order to act in accordance with divine will. If you stray even a fraction from the divine will, you will be off the path. In Aikido, you must know yourself and study the true form of the universe. Never forget the one source of things; understand the underlying principles of life; comprehend the eternal laws; and create marvelous techniques that radiate light.

From one source, the spiritual and material dimensions emerged, giving body and animation to the universe, resulting in the evolution and maintenance of the great Way of the Universal Spirit. All things in heaven and earth are as one family. Past, present, and future are all contained within our life, within our breath; this is what should guide us and purify us as we seek optimal unity. Those who practice *takemusu* [creative martial valor] must never forget the single source of things and always maintain their integrity. Aikido illuminates the inner workings of existence and is a Way based on the discernment of divine principles and divine laws.

In Aikido, the techniques are constantly changing, for change and adaptability are part of the essence of Aikido. I am always training and studying in that spirit, constantly altering the techniques according to the circumstances. Aikido has no forms. It has no forms because it is a study of the spirit. It is wrong to get caught up with forms. Doing so will make you unable to respond with the proper finesse. In Aikido, we first purify our spirits; second, we must set aright our hearts. When using the body we must employ the material dimension but must never lose our focus on the spiritual. At present, our everyday lives are materialistic, but we need a system that harmonizes the material and spiritual, the alpha and omega. The spiritual must control the material.

In today's world, we must foster harmony—every day, all the time. We are scientists of the spirit, but we need concrete results. We have a physical body, but it is not good to think of it as pure matter. Physical power always has a limit.

This world of ours is seeking spiritual salvation. Japan has a role to play in this process, and we must rise up to the challenge. We have been entrusted with a mission. This is clear from Shinto mythology—Japan is said to be a nation of unlimited creativity. Use that creative spirit freely in your body. People all over the globe are eagerly searching for the same thing.

In any endeavor, it is essential to activate your inner spirit. The world is undergoing drastic change. In order to meet those challenges, I practice Aikido. In that spirit, let us all study and train together.

In Shinto cosmology, the god *Takeminakata* [raw animal power] symbolizes activation and a tremendous outpouring of energy. That tremendous explosion of force gave birth to all things and fosters the spirit of bravery. Next comes the symbol of gravitational power, the god *Ooyamanui* [god of the lofty mountains]. He fosters intelligence. The god of the manifest physical earth is *Ootoko*. He brings things into actual being, makes them concrete. He fosters kindness and sympathy. Our present world—the functioning of many diverse principles—was created by the interaction of the deities *Izanagi* [archetypical male] and *Izanami* [archetypical female].

The universe originated from the point between the states of "existence" and "non-existence." This is the source of *aiki* [creative interaction of energy; universal energy, *chi*]. It is the *aiki* described in the *Kojiki*, the ancient chronicles of Japan. Activation of the four souls [*shikon*, rough soul, peaceful soul, happy soul, mysterious soul] created various powers: love, energy, spiritual science. The words of the gods are actually manifestations of different levels of energy. The two jewels *shiomitsu no tama* [high-tide jewel] and *shiohiro no tama* [low-tide jewel] represent the subtle breath of the great earth. The sacred *kusanagi* [majesty of creation] sword, the truth of the universe, the breath of heaven, the interaction between the sun and moon, the breath of earth—all these elements blend together and enter the human heart. Human beings derive their strength from the

Morihei demonstrating *irimi* in order
to unbalance an opponent.

grace and blessings of the gods. *Misogi* [purification] and *aiki* are much
more than the *shiomitsu* and *shiohiro* jewels. You must perceive all the
jewels of existence—the manner in which all things are tied together—
throughout your six senses, and employ energy freely in order to practice
true *aiki*.

The most important aspect in our study is the divine functioning of
Masakatsu agatsu katsuhayabi. *Masakatsu* means unflinching. *Agatsu* means
unflagging. *Katsuhayabi* is the splendor of victory. This supreme principle
is symbolized by the Shinto deity *Masakatsu katsuhaya hi ame oshihomi
no mikoto*. The guardian angel of *aiki* is *Ame no murakumo kuki samuhara
ryu-o*, the deity who represents the world's highest virtue.

Each person must cleanse his or her own heart and set aright his or
her thoughts. We must eliminate all war and fighting from our world.

This divine task we call *odo*. *O* is true emptiness; *do* is settled meditation. It is easy to say "keep your mind set in firm meditation on true emptiness" but very difficult to actually put it into practice. We must practice and forge ourselves so that our noble actions resound throughout the universe. We need to establish heaven on earth. *Ame no murakumo kuki samuhara ryu-o* is the guardian deity of the Ueshiba clan; because of that relationship I was born with that guardian deity in my blood. I am nothing more than a messenger who spreads that god's teaching. I participate in the exalted activities of salvation—to refine one's character, establish solid families, and create a better world.

From ancient times it has been said, "*Bu* is divine." *Bu* is a path established by the gods that is true, good, and beautiful. It was formulated according to divine rules and is the noble path of justice. It is the path for all true people to follow. At the beginning of the world, water, fire, heaven, and earth radiated from the divine light. From *ichirei shikon* [one spirit, four souls] water and fire emerged, existence took shape through the interaction of energy and matter, and the link between body and mind (of all things) was established. It is the spirit that guards and guides the physical form. This belief is an old saying. If we link ourselves to *bu* and foster a sincere *bu* spirit, that spirit will make our bodies good and beautiful, according to the ideal. Again, from ancient times many sages have said, "*Bu* is the root of all things." For example, the writings of such masters as Iizasachoisai [1387–1488; founder of the Tenshin Shoden Katori Shinto Ryu] state that strategy [*bu*] is the source of the Confucian teachings.

Budo is based on the understanding of universal principles, the union of man and god, and the linking of the divine, humans, and subtle energy; this has been so from the beginning of time, and *bu* is the single-minded manifestation of that spirit. This is the origin of the *bu* mind.

In Aikido everything emerges from the energy of *sho* (pine), *chiku* (bamboo), and *bai* (plum blossom). In Shinto terminology, these three energies are known as *ikumusubi* [initial creativity], *tarumusubi* [completing creativity], and *tamatsumemusubi* [fulfilled creativity].

The plum blossom represents the northwest, where the law is heard. It

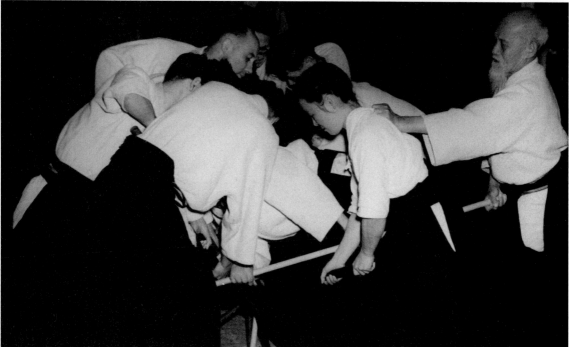

Morihei demonstrating evasion techniques against group attacks.

symbolizes teaching. It is the Floating Bridge of Heaven [rainbow bridge that connects heaven to earth]. The plum blossom is represented by a triangle. The pine has no back or front, so it is called *katsuhayabi*. The teaching of the pine is that of *Miroku* [Buddha of the future; establishment of heaven and earth]. It manifests the *su* seed-syllable [see chapter 5]. *Su* is the source of all, the noble heart and noble form of existence. The pine is represented by the square. In Shinto cosmology this is explained by the creation of physical existence. The expelled breath of *Izanagi* and *Izanami* became air and water and rose, filling heaven and manifesting as a triangular energy. Right in the center of that energy is *budo*, the energy of your own spirit. All spirit is contained there. I often use the example of a combined image of the circle, triangle, and square. These images can also represent the sword and spear. The plum blossom represents the three gods of creation. The triangle image represents the triangular stance of *budo*, which is an invincible, unbreakable posture. The bamboo represents the appropriate use of energy; it is the energy of the Shinto deity *Susano-o* [god of valor and courage], known as the *budo king of strength*.

These three elements are also symbolized by the red jewel, the white jewel, and the crystal-clear jewel. In Shinto cosmology, this is symbolized by *shiomitsu no tama* (red), *shiohiro no tama* (white element), and *kaze no tama* (crystal-clear/union of male and female). We must practice *misogi* in accordance with the exalted virtue of the wind and water. All the pollution accumulated over the years can be washed away by *misogi*. Without *misogi* nothing can be created, nothing can be set aright. In Shinto mythology, this is described as: "The peach tree bears fruit in the southeast." [The peach is a powerful weapon used by the gods to drive away threats.] That peach fruit is said to be *Ookamuzumi no kami* [peach god who protects and nourishes agriculture].

I am always training to establish a dojo of *sho chiku bai*, to bring the spirit of Japan to perfection. Today, many different ways of thinking and lifestyles are being made available to us, and our national character will gradually change, but the essential nature of Japan must not be lost. Aikido is a manifestation of the divine techniques of *odo*. The entire nation of Japan owes its origin to *misogi*. Following the interaction of

Izanagi and *Izanami*, all things were born and animated. Everything was created through *misogi*, and that led to the discovery of Aikido.

Aikido has no forms. Long ago, I earnestly learned *budo* from many outstanding teachers, but on December 14, 1940, around 2:00 o'clock in the morning when I was performing *misogi*, I suddenly forgot every martial art technique I had learned. All of the techniques handed down from my predecessors appeared completely anew. Now they were not just techniques but rather vehicles for the cultivation of life, knowledge, virtue, and good sense.

Then I felt I had a mission in life:

> How beautiful
> this form of
> heaven and earth
> created from the Source—
> we are all members of one family

The entire world is like a single family under one roof, and there is not one outsider. Let us create a prosperous and happy heaven on earth as quickly as we can. Always think like this. Let us join hands and seek harmony; join hands with me, and let us stand together. We must no longer fight; fighting is terribly dangerous. We must eliminate fighting and war from our world. We need techniques of harmony. I was born into a politician's home, and I know first hand how much politicians like to argue and compete. Such conflict is no good. Instead, we must follow the way of the gods. We have no other choice. We need to discern the true workings and true laws of all the divine principles of this wonderful universe. Each one of us must cleanse his or her own heart and set aright one's thoughts—if we fail to do this, the world will never improve.

I always think in such a manner, and I vow to work together with all people of the world to make this happen. I have no students. From the start, I want to be friends with all. Everyone is my teacher. If we train together, it will validate my mission. I think of all of you as my benefactors, as my divine patrons who cooperate with me in my mission.

The god of *aiki* is not at all small. It cooperates with all eight million deities of the world. In our training, the three worlds of Manifest, Hidden, and Divine are innately and inherently present.

If you set aright your heart and establish the spirit of harmony, the three worlds of Manifest, Hidden, and Divine will be harmonized, and all the gods and goddesses of the world will be there to help you. Forge your spirit above all. Forget about concerns of what is powerful, what is weak. The physical techniques we practice have a lethal aspect, but focus instead on their healing properties.

I once had a student named Dr. Kenzo Niki who was an expert on the establishment and maintenance of good physical health and diet. We trained together and assisted each other. At the time Dr. Niki was a member of my dojo, I had many students who were older than I was. However, they were a fine bunch, and we all practiced together with no problem. I know that I must complete my mission, and even if I pass away and am reborn, I will always be working, all the time and everywhere, to make the flower of Aikido bloom in this world.

Please join me and let us train together; then each month, each year the techniques will become more refined and we can advance together. There are no set forms or patterns. Heretofore, because the world has been beset with constant wars and battles, there was a need for various strategies and techniques. These are limited to concrete circumstances and are too narrowly focused. If one's spirit is completely receptive, one can adjust and adapt to any contingency, so there is no need for set forms. Keep this in mind, and you will be able to respond freely in a miraculous manner. I like to talk about the Way of the Gods (Shinto), but the teachings of Buddha are also worthy. We can say that the Manifest realm is that of science, the Hidden realm is that of Buddha, and the Divine realm is that of the gods (*Kami*). Everyone in this world of ours has different principles and spirits that guide them—let's employ them all!

In this path, you must first stand on the Floating Bridge of Heaven [rainbow bridge that connects heaven to earth]. Those who do not stand there cannot perform *aiki*. For this we have a saying: "In three thousand worlds a single plum flower blossoms." [That is to say, seize the chance to reform the world.] In Shinto cosmology, *Izanami* and *Izanagi* stood on the Floating Bridge of Heaven and created the world. In a similar sense, we should (re-)create the world, make all things anew, each time we practice Aikido. Such techniques of unlimited creativity are known as *takemusu* [valorous creativity]. All the *kototama* [seed-syllable] sounds flow from the Floating Bridge of Heaven, reverberate through the universe, and come to reside with our own individual bodies. Human beings are a reflection of the spirit world.

In Aikido, we never focus on our opponent's hands. It is not necessary to focus on the opponent or his posture at all. Look beyond the physical form. Use your spiritual sensibilities. The deity *Ame no murakumo kuki samuhara ryu-o* is within all the techniques of Aikido.

Su is the parent sound that gave birth to the seventy-five *kototama*, out of which phenomena were created. This means the world was created harmoniously without contention and warfare. The grand design of the universe can be determined scientifically.

Aiki is the jewel that resonates throughout the universe—the entire universe, not just bits and pieces of it. Educators and elders must take the initiative and truly practice *budo*. This course of action means to study thoroughly—all things of heaven and earth—and link oneself to the core of the universe. We should progress in conjunction with the universe and seek to absorb and encompass all things with each deep breath.

Forge the spirit and set aright the mind. Through *aiki*, our bodies were formed according to universal principles. We breathe and are tied to those universal principles. We are linked to the center of existence. We are bound to peace and unity. Needless to say, we must no longer conduct wars. Fighting will destroy us. Consensus is the key. No harmony means no true strength. If you do not attain true harmony, all your training will be to no avail.

Aikido is the *aiki* of heaven and earth. It existed right from beginning when heaven and earth first emerged. Employ the soundless sound to establish universal principles. It is important to sense the movement of the Floating Bridge of Heaven as it ascends and descends. This is also true of the rotations of our planet earth. Make the inner rhythm and natural flow of things the center of your education. Where is that center? It is in you! If one is not filled with wisdom and enlightenment and permeated with true power, true *aiki* will be difficult to accomplish.

Here is some *kototama* theory: *O* is the sound of the grand design. *Su-u-yu-mu* is Honosawake Island [the place believed to be the ground of being]. *Aiki* is the harmonizing principle that ties the elements of the world together. It unifies the spirit. It binds things as one. However, people do not understand these concepts, so our world is in danger. From *su*, *u* emanates as the world is brought into being. It emerges from the navel. It spirals forth from that point. One's own *kikai tanden* [physical/spiritual center of a human being] is directly linked to the universe.

The *kototama su u a o u e i* emerge and resound through the universe. For *ame*, heaven, we have *a* (self) and *me* (revolve). The name of the god *Ikiizanainarabu*, which means the individual self has a connection to all other things, is spiritually tied to all dimensions of the life force. Then why is it that the people of the world cannot live in harmony? It is because there are too many conflicting perspectives in this world, and we must try to bridge all the different gaps in thinking.

Aiki fosters the spirit of harmony throughout the world. I speak as a member of the Japanese race and as a member of the family of humankind. We must bring all people of this world together so that they can live in harmony. In present-day Japan, there is still much confusion, much agitation. We need to improve the situation as quickly as possible by peacefully advocating friendship and unity among all people of the world.

Japan must take the lead in this task. Start with self-improvement, and then put one's household in order. After that, work to improve conditions in one's nation and strive to establish harmony throughout the world. The mission of Aikido is to harmonize and protect the three worlds of Manifest, Hidden, and Divine.

From ancient times there have been three sacred regalia in our nation: sword, mirror, and jewel. These are not physical objects but the virtues of bravery, wisdom, and humanity. These are three virtues that every human being treasures in his or her heart. Training in Aikido teaches us how to manifest those three treasures in ourselves. If we look back on history, from the age of the gods to the present, we see that we must be enlightened about human nature. To be enlightened means to learn about one's existence, to perceive one's true nature, to understand where one has come from, to realize the things one must do, to know one's self, and to discover one's mission in life. If we look back on the past, we see that all great human beings accomplished these feats; there is no greater happiness and good fortune than this.

All that is bright and good in this world is due to the virtue of the divine, a virtue present from the beginning. Throughout history, we have been part of the grand design, and we have never been cut off from the source of life, not for an instant. It is essential to find one's true nature.

The Aikido I practice is a path that shows the way, a path where one can forge body and mind. It is not a path used to strike and harm others, or to cut them down with evil weapons.

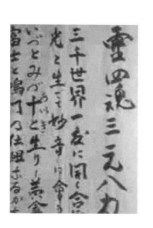

In my life, I have had experience in more than thirty different martial arts, beginning with Yagyu Ryu body techniques; following that I had training in the Shinyo Ryu, the Kito Ryu, the Daito Ryu, the Shinkage Ryu, and so on. However, Aikido is not merely a composite of the various techniques I learned. It depends entirely on *ki* [vital energy]; it is a free flow that follows the waves of the spirit. Keep your spirit healthy; let it sport freely in unison with *aiki*. Aikido is a method to cure the world's sickness. Abandon all self-centered thoughts and petty desires to function freely.

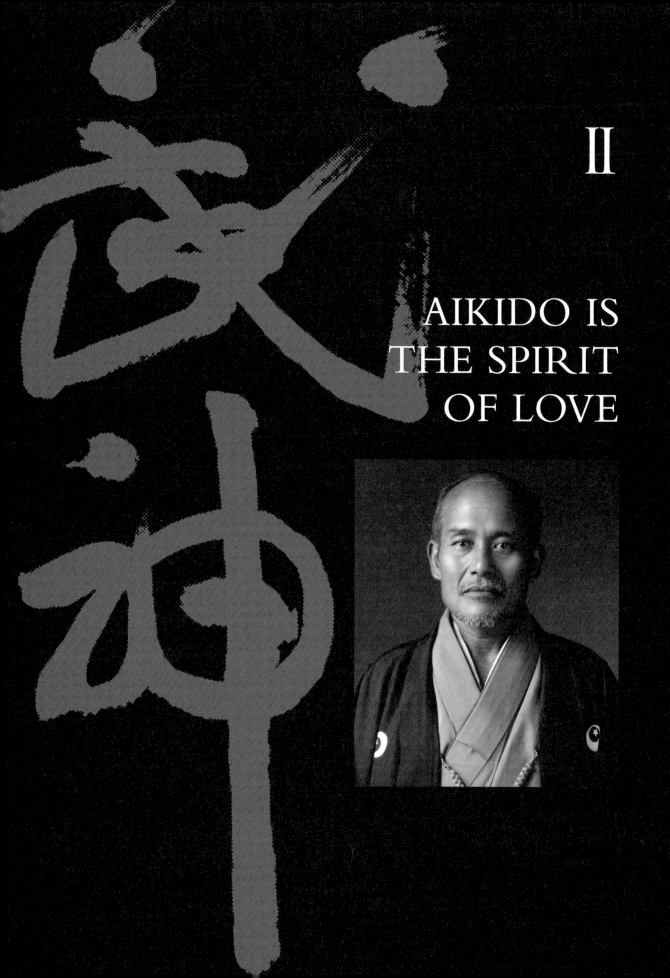

II

AIKIDO IS THE SPIRIT OF LOVE

The secret of Aikido is to expel all maliciousness in one's heart, to attune oneself to the movement of the cosmos, and to unite oneself to the universe. Those who understand the secrets of Aikido have the universe within themselves and can proclaim boldly: "I am the Universe!"

If you ask if our techniques are "fast" or "slow," you will find that time has no existence in Aikido. The speed that transcends time is *Masakatsu agatsu katsuhayabi*. In these three elements the life force and its unlimited adaptability are contained.

How is it possible to expel all evil within, to purify our hearts, and to attune oneself to the movement of the cosmos?

First of all, you must believe that your individual mind and the universal mind are the same. What is the universal mind? Above and below, in the four directions, in past and present, the universal mind has been contained in one grand ideal: love.

Love never fights. Love has no enemies. Anything that makes enemies or creates contention is not the universal mind.

Those who have not united with the universal mind cannot put themselves in tune with the movement of the universe. The arts of war created by human beings for the purpose of warfare are not true *budo*.

True *budo* has no enemies. True *budo* is the manifestation of love. Love

Morihei demonstrating the *kokyu* posture.

never kills; love nourishes. Love brings all things to fruition. Love is the guardian angel of all beings; if there is no love, nothing can be accomplished. Aikido is the embodiment of love.

Techniques used for fighting, for determining victory or defeat, are not true *budo*, because true *budo* is *Masakatsu agatsu katsuhayabi*—it is invincible. It is invincible because it does not contend with anything. Victory means to utterly defeat the mind of contention that exists within. My mission is to teach how to accomplish that feat.

All living beings originate and are manifested by love. Aikido is the purest expression of that love. It is a means to bring all people of this world together. In order to bring people together, to unite human beings with the divine, to co-evolve, we need to tap into the unlimited creative power of existence. *Bu* helps us do this. Etymologically, *bu* means "to stop the spear," and that is what a true warrior strives to do. A true warrior is always conscious of his noble duty to create an enlightened world. This is harmony. A single tiny human being contains the immense universe.

Human beings indeed contain the entire universe with their bodies, but each individual needs to realize the principle of "return to the one." The expression "return to the one" is the key to realization.

This manifold universe functions according to love, but all the shapes and forms we see are in fact just aspects of the one. All the different aspects of human nature, too, are universal manifestations of love. Be aware of these principles when you act, even in such mundane, everyday acts as eating. Food is a gift from the universe. No, in a sense food *is* the universe. Everything on earth functions according to love, and in fact all things are just different aspects of a single body and universal mind. Everyone should understand their mission in life and bring harmony into fruition. Aikido is the best way to manifest the true universal mind of harmony.

Aiki is activated by the cosmic resonance of the spirit of the universe's grand design. Utilize the cosmic resonance to generate unlimited power, to discern the universe, to return to the heart of the universe, to become the universe. Evolve in cooperation with the universe. The grand design of the universe exists within you and shapes your true form.

Another *kokyu* form.

The cosmic resonance of the spirit of the universe enables you to unify mind and body. By extension, that spirit can bring the hearts of all people of the world together. It can give the world peace and unity, not war and contention. We need peace and harmony. We need *aiki*. Those who strive to bring peace and unity to the world are true human beings hoping to perfect human nature through *aiki*. It is important to always foster the qualities of energy, wisdom, virtue, and health.

In order to master utilizing the cosmic resonance of the spirit of the universe, you need to set aright your own heart and to establish your true self. For this purpose, we have the *misogi* techniques of Aikido. *Misogi* techniques forge the great spirit of love, protect the divine principles, and give purpose to your life. *Masakatsu agatsu katsuhayabi* is the form we must assume. It reveals the inner principles of this great and beautifully functioning universe. That is because all things originate from one source. Perceive the true nature of the universe, incorporate it within you, make it your base, and open your eyes—that is the grand purpose of the practice of Aikido. Ceaselessly reflect on your training and constantly strive to progress. That will result in unity of body and mind, total harmonization, and continual advancement. Those who train in Aikido will come to discern the inner principles of the universe and understand the importance of returning to the source of *budo*. Aikido enables one to perceive the true nature of existence. Aikido techniques are based on true forms and are thus endlessly adaptable, creative, and able to respond appropriately to any contingency. Be aware of these factors at all times. To grasp these true principles is to realize that the possibilities are unlimited. If you do not know the true forms, you will understand nothing about how the universe operates. The world needs people who really understand how things work.

It is essential to perceive the truth of the universe. As I always say:

> How beautiful
> this form of
> heaven and earth
> created from the Source—
> we are all members of one family

Let us strive to create a wonderful and beautiful world.

The deity *Hayatakemusu* [meaning swiftness and bravery] is inside me, flowing in my veins. It inspires me in the mission to spread Aikido. The great god *Hayatakemusu* is manifest as *Ame no murakumo kuki samuhara ryu-o*. *Ame no murakumo* represents "universal energy" and "cosmic breath." *Kuki* stands for the "generating power of life." It includes all the elemental forces of nature [gravity, electricity, etc.]. It symbolizes the solar system and the waves of energy that form such things as color, taste, and smell. From here, the marvelous functioning of *kototama* works its magic. *Samuhara* is code for the process that rectifies distortions and puts the warped world back on course. Everything in our solar system, and within the human body as well, originates through the interaction of energy. When things are not kept in tune, evil impulses are generated, and disaster results. The purging of all evil impulses by means of the *misogi* that is based on heavenly truth is what I mean by the term *samuhara*. It is the process of promoting world peace. It is what I call the true path of *bu*.

The great god *Sarutahiko* [deity who shows the way] instructed me: "Ponder this deeply, and use your guardian angel [*Ame no murakumo kuki samuhara ryu-o*] to become a messenger of *takemusu*."

This valorous path is not for destroying humans with weapons and brute strength or for obliterating the world with bombs; it is for setting aright universal *ki*, for promoting world peace, for nurturing all things, and for fostering life. It is a path for forging the spirit, for nurturing life, and it relies on the power of life. These thoughts are always present in my mind and body.

From the love in the center of the great god *Mototsumioyasume o kami* [meaning the creator of all], heat and light developed, generating a tremendous power. This power is a divine force—it is *takemusu*, what I call the great god *Hayatakemusu*. This god is a manifestation of universal love, possessing the power to both create and destroy. The path of *takemusu no bu* is none other than the harmonization of heaven, earth, and humankind through the power of love.

Aiki is unification and co-evolution of spirit and body. Aikido is a manifestation of that truth. Through the power of love all things are gathered together, all things are harmonized. We must establish humanity and love everywhere in this world. If there is anger and hatred, we must pacify it.

A warrior is called a "samurai" because he or she follows the path of life, not because he or she expertly wields a sword to cut people down.

Polish your spirit and body, become a pillar of the nation, and advance the cause of peace.

In the past, the martial arts were mistakenly believed to be for the taking of human life; Aikido, on the contrary, is for the saving of human life. Aikido is a vehicle that protects human life. To practice Aikido is not to kill others. I came to understand that *ai* (harmony) is in fact *ai* (love): Aikido, "Way of Harmony," is really Aikido, "Way of Love." What I mean by the term *aiki* is fundamentally different from the way ancient martial artists understood it. They saw *aiki* as an effective martial technique. I see it as a function of love. Please think about this carefully.

As I said before, Aikido has nothing to do with brute strength, weapons, or war. It is the Art of Peace. Love is the essence of the divine. Love, cosmically and individually, makes the world what it is. Our path is the universal path; to forge one's mind and body on this path is the forging of the divine. Implement this, develop it into an irresistible force, and unify the world.

The three worlds of Manifest, Hidden, and Divine must be harmonized. The human race must come together in peace. It is the responsibility of Aikido to create a joyful and beautiful world. True valor is to promote world peace, to create heaven on earth. That is our path, the great way of peace and harmony.

Bring all races of the world together, unite god and man in both spirit and in body, without violence or harm, and there will be unlimited progress. A real warrior puts an end to all conflict and keeps people from resorting to arms to settle disputes. That is the mission of a warrior. A warrior strives to create inner and outer harmony, unity, and peace throughout the world. The warrior knows that human beings contain the entire universe within them. That is the ultimate principle, the rationale that guides their actions. To enact the peace and unity of the universal mind is the purpose of Aikido.

Since all things function according to love, all things are in effect one body, one universal mind. The gods and humankind are one. Everyone has a role to play in bringing this grand design to fruition. The cosmos consists of myriad forms, countless shapes, but they are all just aspects

"Rowing the boat" *kokyu* form.

of a single reality. All things, human beings too, are just different expressions of the function of love. Act with firm conviction that this is true. Love is the animating source of this universe; all actions are a function of love. Aikido is the purest and most direct expression of this truth. It is the original path that constantly acts to create peace and harmony among all peoples and cultures of the world.

Aikido nourishes life as the manifestation of love. This functioning of love shapes the universe. It protects, purifies, and completes all things. The exalted mission of Aikido is to nourish and bring all things to perfection. The universe sows innumerable seeds, and these seeds sprout with an irresistible energy. This life force, this incredible vitality that supports the cosmos, this manifestation of love in this world, this unification of the Manifest, Hidden, and Divine, this continual mission to permeate our being with harmony is what is called Aikido.

Do not rely on your unrefined physical senses to look at the world. Buddhism advocates purification of the sense organs in order to perceive the manifest universe the way it really is. To understand the physical world, your sense organs must be clear and untainted. Disharmony disrupts and causes confusion. Creating disharmony is the world's worst sin. Polish your mind, refine your senses, and your spirit will shine. Your senses will shine. Your pure spirit will surface. You will be able to utilize beams of light to become spiritually sensitive. You will be infinitely creative. You will be able to see both the inner and outer aspects of existence. You will understand that your self is not something separate from that which appears outside. The practice of Aikido is all about this, and it does not formulate hard and fast rules.

> Sun, earth, moon
> harmonized perfectly
> on the bridge
> above the vast sea
> the mountain echo calls me

From the void fifty, then seventy-five *kototama* reverberate through the universe creating these techniques. Keep in mind that all things originate in the void, and advance in your training. The great parent of creation, the great spirit of love, emanates from the seed-syllable *su*:

> From the exalted sun
> seventy-five sounds
> were born,
> teaching the
> way of *aiki*

This indicates that the techniques all evolved from the seventy-five *kototama*; each individual being in fact has evolved from these vibrations, and

Morihei demonstrating the *hasso jo* posture.

one needs to develop the ability to function freely within one's body.

I feel that all of you are members of my family. It is not my duty to act as your teacher; it is my honor to work in conjunction with all of you. If we work together in unison we will be able to protect everyone and guard our legacy. To do this, one must first know oneself; then one can develop understanding of all things. Because you exist, the universe exists; in that sense, you are the universe. You will then clearly understand your original nature. You will understand your mission in life. This is not something I accomplish as a separate entity. I can do this because I am part of the universe. You must know that all of us are like this.

You must know that your being and the stuff of the universe are the same. You are a child of the universe. In religious terms, you are a child of god, so you should act accordingly to prevent disorder in this world. You should protect and nourish all forms of life.

Aikido is an extension of the universal life force. It is a manifestation of the grand design of the cosmos from the vastness of space down to the smallest plants and animals. Aikido is the way that shows us how to appreciate these truths.

Economics is the basis of society. When the economy is stable, society develops. In our nation, the ideal has been to combine the spiritual and material aspects of economy. In traditional Japan, the best commodities to trade in were honesty and love. *Budo* is the same—it begins with love, summoning first the best qualities of a human being.

All of the great masters of the past taught us how to echo the actions of heaven and earth, how to harmonize ourselves with heaven and earth, and how to live a peaceful and pleasant life. Aikido provides us with the strings that can tie all things together through the power of life.

The root of Japanese *bu* is love. Love shapes all things in this world. Culture and science are derived from the great spirit of love. All human beings are held together by the cords of love as they stand between heaven and earth.

There are many paths that lead to the top of Mount Fuji, but there is only one summit—love. There are many different methods of training, but the goal is the same. In Japan, *bu* is not for war, fighting, or contention.

Rather, it is a path that sees all human beings as brothers and sisters.

Let me tell you about a dream I recently had. I was in the dreadful realm of warring spirits, and I had to fight furiously for my survival. I had to be number one. I had a vision of my face—it was hideously ugly, totally dark, and distorted by terrible anger. I battled my way to a wide river. The water was turgid and muddy. As I wondered how I could cross the raging water, a large plank came floating down the river toward me, and I got on it. Five or six of my disciples were already on the plank, and the spirits I was fighting with also got on board. Due to the heavy load, the plank began to sink. Two of my disciples, one named Funabashi, and then another named Yukawa, sacrificed themselves by leaping off the plank into the river, and the rest of us made it safely to the other shore. Those two sacrificed themselves for my sake.

When we arrived on the other shore, it was full of green fields. The others rested there. I was the only one who continued on the path. I kept moving toward the light, shedding tears of gratitude as I walked on alone. To follow this noble path you must not desire anything else. When you are liberated from desire, you are truly free. I was in a world where everyone was liberated from desire.

Aikido is not a bunch of words, it is *misogi*:

> Learn the structure of
> the *ki* jewels
> and follow the way of
> *misogi* techniques—
> this is *odo no kamuzawa*

Misogi in Aikido is to set aright the spirit. I especially hope that young people will practice this path every day. Let us all follow the divine techniques of *odo* for the sake of the world. The divine techniques of *odo* originated when *Izanagi*, *Izanami*, and *Takamimusubi* created the earth. The great god *Izanami* represents the spirit that animates our earth. Before there was heaven, before there was earth, when there was nothing, *aiki* sprang forth to bring the universe into existence. *Misogi* shows the way this was accomplished. The three worlds of Manifest, Hidden, and Divine flow in and out of Ueshiba. *Misogi* techniques purify us. My Aikido cooperates with all the eight million gods and goddesses of the world.

Aikido has no form. *Su* is the spiritual seed-syllable that is the basis of *misogi*. This universe was brought into being by the power of *su*. Each human spirit is a direct spark of the universal spirit. Aikido is based on natural law of the spirit, not artificially constructed rules. Aikido must never be separated from the teaching of love. If there is no spark of life, true power cannot emerge. Water and fire interact to create matter. I use the image of the Floating Bridge of Heaven to symbolize the primordial act of creation.

This very body of ours is a golden cauldron for the alchemy of the spirit. Our speech is a reverberation of the *kototama*. *Kototama* are the pillars of heaven. Aikido links us to the world beyond form. If we respond to a physical form, it is already too late. Within your breath is an actual physical expression of your body. Aikido is the red jewel, the white jewel, and the crystal-clear jewel. The crystal-clear jewel is akin to the essence of air. All this theory is important, but above all, Aikido must be put into actual practice.

When the cosmos emerged, there was tremendous overflow of energy and space. The very center of this creative explosion is what we call, in Shinto terminology, *Ookami* [great spirit]. The spirit of this single point emerged from the absolute virtues of humaneness and love.

This divine heart of absolute love and goodness has one purpose: to create a beautiful, pleasant, and safe world. All truth, the entire scope of heaven and earth, *kototama*, the sun and moon, all deities, all beings, all things are manifest to fulfill this purpose. Activation of this great spirit of humaneness and love is the obligation of Aikido. Animating and nourishing the life of the universe that is within each being is another purpose for Aikido.

Aiki can be explained by the interaction of triangle, circle, and square. A circle with a dot in the center represents stillness and fostering of the spirit. It is the circular flow that creates myriad techniques. The square represents unlimited transformation. It acts like the moon, sometimes

Morihei demonstrating
a *jo* strike.

out in the open, sometimes hidden, in this present world. When it is hidden, it represents the one source; when it is out in the open, it reveals the infinite variations possible. A triangle generates the power of *ki*, and a triangular stance is the invincible posture of a warrior. Train in the three patterns of triangle, circle, and square and it will generate light, heat, and power. It will give you power that is irresistible. Those with such irresistible power will be able to grasp the natural, absolute love of heaven and earth and always display the warmth of goodness and love.

Aikido is the true and essential path that unites space and time, animates all human beings, and nourishes them with love. Do not forget this. Follow and fulfill your mission. In our Japanese culture, we believe that true victory is the victory over oneself. From time immemorial the sun, moon, and stars have been performing their functions in perfect symphony, without collision or disruption, bestowing the blessings of love upon existence. It is the task of a human being to train in *aiki*, to manifest love and goodness, and to bring god and man together.

Those leaders who understand how heaven and earth work should take the initiative to build a beautiful pure land, a stable society where human beings can live long and peaceful lives. This is Aikido.

Aikido is a double-edged sword of *ki*. *Ki* is the heart of things. The truth of this world utilizes the great technique of the spirit that transforms light and heat. The double-edged sword consists of the essence of the seventy-five *kototama*; it is the transformation of *ki* that gives birth to 10,000 forms.

Aikido is based on the absolute love found in nature. The body is a triangle, the circle is in the exact center. The interaction of the triangle and circle is bodily manifest as *ikumusubi*. This force sustains life and links emptiness with form; it is the marvelous path of endless creativity. Aikido enables us to truly unify emptiness and form. In human beings, Aikido ties emptiness and form together with love, completely transforming and elevating our spirits to the highest level.

> As soon as the
> Demon Snake
> attacks
> I am already behind it
> guiding it with love

In the summer of 1925 I was walking in my garden. The earth began to tremble, and golden vapor welled from the earth, enveloping my body. I felt transformed into a golden being. Simultaneously, I felt light as a feather in mind and body. I could understand the language of the birds. I understood the meaning of creation. At that instant I realized, "the source of *bu* is god's love—the spirit of protection for all things." Tears of joy streamed down my cheeks. Since then I have viewed this entire world as my family—the sun, moon, and stars are my friends too. Fame, fortune, status no longer meant anything to me.

I realized an important truth: *budo* is not to topple opponents with brute force or weapons, or to destroy the world with war. True *budo* is to set things aright, to establish world peace, to nourish and protect all things. That is the purpose of my training in *budo*: to nourish, protect, and foster all life with the power of god's love.

III

TAKEMUSU
AIKI

From ancient times, it has been said, "*Bu* is divine." *Bu* is the divine way established by the gods, and it symbolizes all that is true, good, and beautiful in this world. It is based on divine principles, and it guides us according to those dictates. It is the beam of light that creates real human beings.

At the onset of creation, water, fire, heaven, and earth separated and the physical universe emerged from the power of *ichirei shikon* and the interaction of water and fire. The body guards the spirit, and vice versa. The spirit guards the eight bodies.

Bu principles should guide us. If you practice *bu*, you will foster the spirit of *bu*. The spirit of *bu* unifies mind and body in a true, good, and beautiful manner. From ancient times, wise people have proclaimed, "*Bu* is the foundation of all things." Japanese *bu* is derived from the virtuous glory of the sword, the mirror, and the jewel. It is a gift of the gods, the principle that unites man with the divine and fosters single-minded bravery. *Bu* is the source of life.

After the initial act of creation, light and heat emerged, and through the tremendous power generated by the interaction of water and fire, the solar system developed. The universal spirit formed the *kototama*; the *kototama* always envelop us, inside and outside, and lead us along the path of sincerity, show us how to harmonize heaven and earth. The energy of *bu*

Morihei demonstrating a seated pin.

binds the universe and unites the inner and outer worlds; it manifests the virtues of bravery, wisdom, love, and empathy. That virtue is symbolized by a crystal-clear mirror that reflects good and evil acts, and illumines all.

The sword beams with light; it shines as the eight-sided jewel. Buddhists call this jewel *nyoi-hoju* [gem capable of granting every wish]. Shintoists call it *shiomitsu* or *shiohiru*, the indestructible red and white jewels. The blending of the universe and the breath is a state where there is only the divine; this is represented by the crystal-clear mirror. It reflects all things and is a divine sword that makes the outer and inner worlds as one. That is the sword of purification, a divine instrument that pacifies and guides the world.

Aiki is the inner principle of existence. We must be convinced of this special teaching, not just passively accept it. "Steal" it because it is so valuable. The teaching cannot be forced upon you, but it is our task to make it available.

Phenomena themselves are the great teachings of *budo*. Although phenomena manifest the divine on the surface, and their light permeates heaven and earth, few comprehend this. Unfortunately, it is often our rulers who have the poorest understanding of this concept, and act badly. Each of them only thinks about their own little sphere of interest, and this causes endless competition and strife. Everything becomes based on greed. If your heart is pure, you can act in a detached manner, but I know that is much easier said than done.

Do not think that the gods are above us. This eternal universe is held together by gravity—the descending of *ki*—and the marvelous power of heaven and earth is sustained by the interaction of gravitational forces. This was accomplished by Aikido. Aikido is completely different from the old *budo*. This does not mean that we should abandon the old *budo*. We should incorporate them and infuse them with new life. Each individual has his own role to play, his own spirit to refine. Become divine yourself, and work for the good of this world. The divine is in heaven, the divine is in earth, the divine is within you. There will come a time when you will become a *Kami*, a divine spirit, and selflessly work for the benefit of all beings.

From the divine mind of one source, two elements arose and manifested all things. This is the beginning of science.

Training in *budo* involves much more than just technique. *Budo* provides you with a solid foundation that will help you be successful in any endeavor. *Budo* is the base that enables you to advance. It creates opportunities. It is a vehicle that gives us many possibilities. *Budo* forms our character. Always strive to train and develop the *budo* spirit.

The grand design of the universe is no other than the great way of *bu*. It is the ideal way of universal harmony and promotes the establishment of heaven on earth. The warriors of old were careful not to defile the divine heart. There is no need to cast off the old ways completely; one just needs to train with a fresh spirit each day. Do not violate the traditional values or besmirch the grand principles of *budo*; rather, refresh and renew the *budo* spirit in each generation. Keep the bright mirror of *budo* clean.

Bu is a mirror to the world. *Bu* acts as the world's compass. *Bu* represents all that is good in the Japanese spirit. *Bu* is action, not words—it makes the principles of heaven concrete on earth. Utilize the mind and

Morihei demonstrating an old-style
pinning technique.

body you have received from heaven to promote true democracy in this
world and universal peace. This is the mission of Aikido.

Aikido is to make each day anew. Remove the old garments of *budo*,
but continue to progress and develop in the traditional spirit. Use *budo*
to learn the true nature of heaven and earth and the manner in which
heaven and earth operate; train sincerely in *budo* to build a single-minded
spirit and a healthy body.

The present world is chaotic because people have forgotten that all of
us come from one source. The subtle and marvelous interaction of spirit
and matter gave birth to and sustains the cosmos. The universe evolved
with animation and form from one source; all of us are in fact members
of the same family, one body, in which the past, present, and future
live and breathe within each one of us. Realize this profound truth, and

you can be an asset for others, a leader who tirelessly works to heal the world's ills and advance the cause of unity.

When you practice *bu* do not forget that all things emerge from one source, and adhere to the principle that love generates more love. At present, the material economy is well developed but spiritual science lags behind. If we can unite the best elements of material and spiritual science, the world will be much improved, war will disappear, and peace will be established. Aikido must function in harmony with the dictates of heaven. Physical *budo* never leads to perfection, and brute strength has limited application.

True *budo* is the clarification of all the dimensions of matter and spirit; it generates a robust, pure, and indestructible energy. In Aikido, first we must know ourselves; next, we must know that all elements of the universal are contained within us; then we must discern the true nature of the cosmos. Do this, understand the laws of nature, and you will be radiant, able to execute marvelous techniques.

Upon reflection, we can see that Aikido is the source of Japanese *budo*, following and illuminating universal principles. Aikido unifies heavenly truth, earthly truth, and material truth; it is for those who seek harmony and enlightenment; it is for those who are single-minded in their quest; it is for those who continually polish the spirit; it is the way that lies beyond words and theories; it lies at the center of the resonance of heaven and earth.

In the martial arts there are various shouts. For example, *"ei," "yaa," "too," "ha,"* and so on. There are many more possible shouts than these four sounds; they are all derived from *kototama* theory. These *kototama* sounds are based on deep breathing and the rhythm between the voice and the mind. The sound "flies out" when a technique is executed; its quality expresses the extent of one's mind/body unity. When voice, body, and mind are unified, excellent techniques result. *Aiki* is to train to develop the splendid power that is generated by the unity of spirit and body. This unity of voice, body, and mind is the essence of traditional martial arts training, practiced over and over—such concentrated spirit is the pillar of *budo*. Follow the example of all the great masters, martial

Morihei demonstrating an evasion technique against a group attack in the original Hombu Dojo.

artists such as Yagyu Jubei [1607–1650, Yagyu Ryu swordsman] and Tsukahara Bokuden [1489–1571, founder of the Kashima Shinto Ryu]; realize that *budo* energy is a blessing of the gods that we need to treat and harness with reverence.

Take the words of these great exemplars to heart and make their teachings part of your being by practicing them every day; harmonize your breath with the breath of heaven and earth. On occasion, we cut with *"ei,"* receive with *"ya,"* and separate with *"too."* When you and your partner are in tune, the *too* separation *kiai* [spirited shout] works well, but if one of the partners has an opening, the *ei* and *ya kiai* will not be effective. In the old days, it was said that when the *ei* and *ya* were harmonized, the *too* separation *kiai* would work. In short, the *kiai* were used to facilitate training without openings or slack. If such training was done in earnest, it would be possible to sense an impending attack and neutralize it immediately with an appropriate technique. This sense is the key to effective throws and pins. Train diligently in the techniques, improve your level, and forge your spirit.

In old-time swordsmanship it was said, "Allow the skin to be cut in order to cut the flesh; let the flesh be cut in order to cut to the bone." That is, sacrifice a cut to your skin or even to your flesh to get close enough to cut to your enemy's bone. However, in today's world we do not want the skin to even get scratched. It is foolish to let yourself get injured—you must control an opponent with your mind, before anyone gets hurt. We need the life-giving sword—the sword that opens us to life possibilities—not a razor-sharp blade that clefts in two. The masters of old practiced that lethal technique, but it is too dangerous (and not necessary) to use today.

Control your opponent by always keeping yourself in a safe, unassailable place. This insight is the most essential element of practice.

Aikido is the true *budo* of Japan. It derives from the teachings of the gods concerning the grand design of the universe. According to Shinto divination theory (*futomani*), the spirits of water and fire emerged to interact and evolve, eventually creating human life. In Aikido, we term this process *odo no kamuzawa*. Aikido is the three-dimensional manifestation

A demonstration by Morihei at
the Japan Industrial Club in 1934.

of universal emptiness. The universe was created through the interaction of principles represented by *Takamimusubi* [centripetal force] and *Kamimusubi* [centrifugal force]; the earth we inhabit was formed by the interaction of the principles represented by *Izanagi* and *Izanami*. They united at the midpoint between existence and non-existence and gave birth to the world. Each human being is in fact a living shrine of these two gods, *Izanagi* and *Izanami*; we are all part of the gods' grand design, participants in the act of creation, and are all responsible for assisting in that great work. The three worlds of Manifest, Hidden, and Divine are within us, activated by water and fire; each and every human being is a miniature universe. It is our duty to make this world a better and more glorious place each day. Know that this is the reason we practice Aikido.

In Aikido we must stand on the Floating Bridge of Heaven.

Masakatsu agatsu katsuhayabi is the core of *takemusu*. These terms are not new, they are mentioned and explained in the *Kojiki* and other ancient chronicles of Japan as the teachings of the gods. We should study these exalted principles every day. All breath originated with the sacred seed-syllable *su* and expanded to fill the four corners of the universe. Our universe from pole to pole overflows with divine spirit and virtue. Try to experience this grand emotion daily. Let the flower of your spirit bloom.

When *sho chiku bai* came together, the state of "in 3,000 worlds a plum blossom opens at once" was realized. This initiated all things, and gave birth to *aiki*. This is also called the Floating Bridge of Heaven. The guardian angel of *takemusu* is *Ame no murakumo kuki samuhara ryu-o* (also known in the spirit world as *Hayatakemusu*). That is the spirit that inspires and guides us in Aikido. Our spirit reflects the divine realm and is activated by *takemusu aiki*. It is essential to put into practice the ethical principles elaborated in the *Kojiki* [and other sacred scriptures of the world].

When the universe was formed, the lighter elements rose and became heaven; the heavier elements descended and became earth. The heavier elements are never going to become lighter elements no matter how many eons pass. This is a fact of nature. While we are here on earth, our spirit is inseparable from the body. That is how human beings are made. Therefore, you must unify spirit and form and harmonize the mind and the body in order to develop a character that is beautiful and radiant. The kingdom of heaven is within; god is love. Never oppose that path of love; protect this world of ours, and let us walk hand in hand along the path of love. This has been the way since the beginning of time.

Bu techniques comprise entering, blending, and restraining movements. These movements involve the entire body. Practice them diligently.

The body is a creation of the universe. The exalted form of *bu* is within the body. It is where power resides. It energizes your spirit. Delusion, maliciousness, and evil all develop when one's spirit is distressed. *Ki* is the life force centered in the body. Depending where this *ki* is located, different things develop. Power must emerge from *ki*.

Those who cannot fill themselves with *ki* and move freely cannot project full strength. Above all, you must find the exact place where the void (*shinku no ki*) and emptiness (*ku no ki*) reside. The universe is suffused with the void. It is the actual source of all things. The world of matter is emptiness. This aspect is what sustains physical existence. Emptiness possesses the supreme power that activates matter. In order to be agile of body with lightning-fast techniques, one must dwell in the void. Emptiness forms the strings of gravitational force. To move freely, you must liberate yourself from this heavy force. If you liberate yourself from the grosser elements and link your movement to the void, effective techniques will emerge.

However, by clinging to the notion of liberation you will encounter problems. Without real liberation you are as good as dead. Just like pulling a bow to its full extent, flood your entire being with the void, and cleanse your soul.

If you purify your spirit, your body will immediately fill with the void and permeate all your sense organs; this creates an ideal state of being that radiates light and love, creates technique and strength. The glory of *aiki* is not simply derived from individual strength and technique; those two elements develop from the grand design of the universe.

The power manifest by *bu* is the combination of technique and light. Set your mind firmly in the center of these two elements. If you have such a stable center, you can move effectively. This center is in your belly. If your belly is centered, your heart will progress in understanding *masakatsu* and *agatsu*. Link yourself to the universe through ceaseless training, and you will be able to perform unlimited techniques.

The eight islands of Japan were created in order and with a distinct purpose. From the northwest matter and mind began; from the northeast physical form took shape.

Matter is female (sword); mind is male (spear). The right foot of *Kuni no tokotachi no kami* (female deity) is in the center to initiate the creative process. Her left foot descends, advancing left (embodying heaven) and right (embodying earth). This embodies the birth of *takemusu aiki*. From the harmonious interaction of heaven and earth the Floating Bridge of Heaven appears. All is seamless existence. This is the palace where the gods reside in perfect repose and accord, the heavenly court (*yahirodono*). In other words, the place where universal truth is revealed and divine dictates are established. *Bu* gives birth to matter and spirit.

Bu is the force that permeates matter and spirit; it is the force that enters, blends with, and controls. It is the force that generates and enacts light, heat, and power.

Everything possesses matter and spirit. This is the way life functions. At birth one is the deity *Minakanushi no kami* [the center of the world]. Next comes *Kuni no tokotachi no kami* (female deity). Heaven descends in the form of the male deity *Toyokumo no kami*.

Left is activation, right is reception; the birth of matter and spirit is female. This act is centered in the spirit of manifold creation (*mochiro*). The right foot advances and steps on the very center of existence. Next the left foot moves, enabling countless variations, and physical adaptability. The left foot forward creates a triangular stance and moves forward a half-step.

The left foot is symbolized by *Toyokumo no kami*, creator of countless variations and unlimited divine forms and divine secrets. It activates life. The right foot must move as *Kuni no tokotachi no kami* (female deity) and represents the grasping of *ki*.

When creation moves from gross spirit to subtle spirit we have:

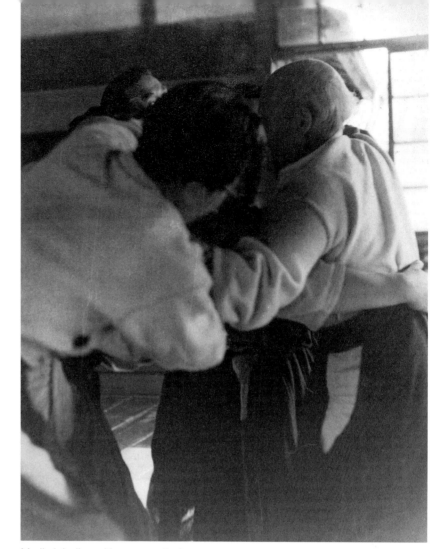

Morihei dealing with a group attack.

Left—*masakatsu*—*Toyokumo no kami* (male deity)

Right—*agatsu*—*Kuni no tokotachi no kami* (female deity)

Katsuhayabi, the combination of left and right, is the foundation of the actual techniques.

From the left, all things evolve according to unlimited *ki*. This is the state of creative vigor and victorious technique. The spirit vibrates and the left side activates dynamic freedom. The left grasps life and death, the right terminates it. This is the divine technique of the left. *Takemusu aiki* determines if a technique emerges or disappears, if there is life or death.

Know that the energy of the four limbs (hands and feet) link us to the four heavens, the eight directions, yin and yang, front and back.

"Living things need rest." Rest is the key to proper living. A square symbolizes that state of repose. All of us have been bestowed with the three treasures and the ten treasures [instruments that heal the sick and resuscitate]. They are within us. They represent the single purpose of creation. They are the reason why heaven and earth were made. It is the aim of the big bang that exploded from the primordial emptiness. This universe is an expression of *ichirei shikon-sangen hachiriki* [one spirit, four souls-three fundamentals, eight powers; a code word for the initial act of creation and the manifestation of existence], a single tremendous entity.

Through the interaction of *aiki*, one becomes *Ame no manaka nushi* and completes the act of creation. We are in fact the universe, and it is our duty to manifest its grand design in our beings. The kingdom of heaven is within us. It is the force that animates us, the divine spark that gives us freedom. Use that force to stand on the Floating Bridge of Heaven, and activate the marvelous functioning of *kototama* by disseminating the red and white blood cells within your body; that will generate light, heat, and power. In extreme terms, boil your blood to produce a sound that summons forth light, heat, and power. In *kototama* theory this is represented by the sound "*u*" (generating the four dimensions of air, liquid, softness, and hardness). Link yourself to *u* and you will be able to display great power. This is the origin of all things, the verdant garden of life.

To repeat: The Floating Bridge of Heaven symbolizes an enlightened state of being; it represents understanding of the grand design of the cosmos. One who knows this truth is able to metaphorically boil his or her blood to generate light, heat, and power and simultaneously pronounce the *kototama* "*o*." The sound *o* represents a person who speaks and acts truly, one who is always standing on the Floating Bridge of Heaven. The Floating Bridge of Heaven stands for the power of love and the manifestation of truth. It emerged from *su-u*; *u* spiraled into spirit and matter to form this world, from the most immense sphere down to the tiniest element. It is the bridge that spans the universe and instructs us in the true nature of the world.

From the initial seed-syllable *su*, *ta ka a ma ha ra* emerged. From these six *kototama* the seventy-five sounds took shape and developed into the universe as an expression of the divine mind. The number of *kototama* reflects the number of essential spirits and patterns in the world.

The transformation of *kototama* is solely dependent on consciousness. This consciousness is the jewel-like strings of the spirit. They are the veins that hold the world together. To discern the nature of sound is the purpose of *kototama* science. To investigate the strings of the spirit is the purpose of the *ho kototama* of all the gods of heaven.

The jewel strings of the spirit already exist, emanating from the spirit, to give voice and color to phenomena; the strings color existence, allowing it to be seen and heard. This is called "nature," a phenomenon that is palpable to the consciousness. There is intellectual knowledge, there is pure emotion, and in fact eight or nine kinds of consciousness; these allow the mind to discern the details of things.

If you do not stand on the Floating Bridge of Heaven, *bu* will never be born. The purpose of *bu* is to give birth to techniques based on the unifying principle originating with the joining of the divine and phenomena, and the generation of love, heat, light, and power.

The Floating Bridge of Heaven is the basis of *takemusu aiki*. Each one of us has to actually stand on the Floating Bridge of Heaven and let the spirit of *bu* permeate and captivate our minds and bodies.

Bu is created by the boiling of the red blood cells in the body. They interact to cause the 1,000 seeds of life to sprout. These are the techniques of science. All of us have been endowed with a mission from heaven to benefit the world; we are sparks of the divine, we were made in god's image. When we implement that mission we are acting like the deities. Our wills, our actions, our glory, our love, our strength, our *bu*, and our words all serve our mission.

The functioning of *ikumusubi*, *tarumusubi*, *tamatsumusubi*, and the *ichirei shikon-sangen hachiriki* is the basis of modern science. It gives structure and purpose to this world.

In the *kototama ta ka a ma ha ra*, *ra* is the sound that initiates actual creation by generating waves of divine atoms. Higher and lower frequency wavelengths form different aspects of the solar system. In Shinto cosmology, we discern four spirits, the *shikon*: rough soul, peaceful soul, happy soul, mysterious soul. This occurred in response to the respected will of *Kuni no tokotachi* and resulted in actualization of the manifest and hidden dimensions of *ichirei shikon-sangen hachiriki*.

The practice sequence: first disseminate the blood within to initiate the *ta ka a ma ha ra* sounds; imagine kindling a fire in your inner shrine, making your entire body an ascending *kototama*. (This is akin to tuning in the messages that are constantly being broadcast on the airwaves but can only be heard if you turn on the machine.) After the entire body congeals into a *kototama*, simultaneously pronounce the seed-syllables and tap in the universal beams of energy; let the self expand into a huge sphere before actually vocalizing the sounds. As the seed-syllables emerge from deep within your being, draw the universe into your body. Your spirit will be suffused with light and completely centered.

Here is an explanation of the *A O U E I* seed-syllables, essential for Aikido practitioners:

Open your mouth wide and from the bottom of your throat, expel the breath. This makes the sound *A*.

A emerges from the water-soul deep within space [as do *O U E* and *I*], creating something from nothing. All fifty sounds are in it, and it circulates through heaven as the three fundamentals. It is nature. No matter how it is vocalized it remains *tokotachi*. *A* in Shinto cosmology is known as *Kuni no tokotachi* (or *Kuni sokunushi no kami*). *Izanami* received this *A* to form the world. As the sound *A* emerges the mouth gradually becomes narrower and the *O* sound occurs.

O arises and gracefully circulates in an upward manner to link earth with heaven. Since the *O* sound is emitted when the lips are symmetrical, it is called *Toyokumo no kami* (or *Kuni no sazuchi no kami*). When the sound *O* is completely pronounced, the mouth closes, the sound *U* is formed.

U floats to the surface. It is motion, vitality, darkness. *U* links upper and lower. In Shinto cosmology *U* is *Ujihi no kami*. If *U* is pronounced strongly it ultimately turns into *SU*. *SU* is the sister deity of *U*, *Suhinchi no kami*. Beneath each respective *Kami* there is a (⟋ ⟍) slash mark. These marks are accents. When *U* is fully vocalized, the tongue reaches the lowest point in the mouth. It is like a post, or the shape made when the eye is turned up. The sound *E* naturally emerges.

E is the placenta of heaven and earth. It forms the limbs and branches of things. It is heaven's mother sound. When *E* is pronounced strongly the tongue turns, making it possible to produce the *RE* sound. That is why the *E* sound is called *Tsunukui no kami* and *Imoikukui no kami*. When the *E* sound is completely expelled from the mouth, the sound *I* naturally occurs.

I, if pronounced strongly, naturally produces the sound *GI*, This is the culmination of all sounds, the father and mother of language. In Shinto cosmology, *I* is called *Ohotonoji no kami* and *GI* is *Otonobe no kami*.

A O U E I are the great vowels that animate language. They bestow life and allow us to vocalize the teachings. When all five mother seed-syllables are present, we worship a state represented by *Odamaru no kami* and *Ayashikone no kami*, the two deities responsible for all language.

When uttered, the virtuous and creative power of *A O U E I* spirals up to the right, and spirals down to the left, creating manifold sounds (and consequently all phenomena) through the combustion of water and fire. This is aptly called the Way of Teaching. There are many students of *kototama* theory, but in Aikido we must actually embody and implement the practice of *kototama*. Thus, pronunciation of *O* leads to the pronunciation of *U*, which in turn activates the blood, summoning forth dynamic power, generating form, light, and heat, and developing the living technique of producing countless sounds. When that sound is linked to the three fundamentals, mind-power (*nenriki*) surfaces, and the head moves up and down while the body and spirit are permeated with that sound.

Every human being is innately connected to a spiritual power with tremendous potential; this power is a function of the seventy-five sounds emanating from one source that activates the cosmos, enlivens the *kototama*, represents the grand design of the universe, and fosters and protects all worlds. It is the great way that nourishes life.

A human is created by *kototama*, with his or her being formed by vibration. This I call the crystal-clear jewel, a function of the one spirit, a manifestation of sound, actualization of the deities that are uttered by one's lips and felt throughout the body. It is our obligation to maintain and protect the legacy of the exalted ancestors of our nation.

In the venerable kingdom of eternity, *takemusu samuhara aiki* generated an outpouring of love and light, red *ki* and the red blood cells bubbled, and the glittering jewels became the true base of existence.

There has been a seamless connection from the age of the gods up to the present day, with human beings standing on the Floating Bridge of Heaven, uttering the secret sounds of the universe. This ideal has now appeared in this world as our *katsuhayabi*.

Meditate on the *Kojiki*. It describes the linking of void and emptiness. The deity *Ame no shiho mimi no mikoto* [=*Masakatsu agatsu katsuhayabi*] descended from the Floating Bridge of Heaven as a messenger of *Amaterasu* [sun goddess]; that deity linked up with the spirit of *samuhara* to incarnate itself in our bodies and souls. This is the *bu* that animates us. The left and right of the Floating Bridge of Heaven are our own left, right, left movement. We are made in god's image, we are guided by *Sarutahiko*, and we can utilize the energy generated by his great powers. Attain the five-sided plate, stand on the Floating Bridge of Heaven, and link yourself to the gods and exalted ancestors.

Aikibudo is intimately connected to the divine principles expressed in the *Kojiki*. Aikido follows those principles and stands on the Floating Bridge of Heaven. *Bu* is a creation of the gods and the cosmos, and it utilizes essential techniques that are created from love, heat, light, and power. Our mission is to manifest the divine mind—display the reality of *bu*—in the Aikido techniques. Oral transmission in Aikido consists of imparting these teachings individually in meaning (mind) as well as intent

Morihei demonstrating a right-angle 90° entry against a straight sword attack.

(body). *Bu* is a living principle. *Bu* consists of scientific techniques. When we become vessels of the divine, when we realize the spiritual mission, the gods are manifest in this very body. Stand amid this world's evil and corruption as a missionary for the art of peace; work tirelessly to restore the balance in society through the power of *misogi*.

Our physical form is made up of a vapor body (*kitai*) and liquid body (*ekitai*). The base of inanimate objects is our own heart. We are sparks of the divine, and the temporary separation from that source empowers us with the freedom to be. Too often, people get attached to the idea of freedom, forget about their divine mission, and become selfish and act willfully. *Misogi* is for purging oneself of those self-centered thoughts, a graveyard, if you will, where the matters of life and death are resolved.

A *budo* dojo can also be thought of as a graveyard where ultimate questions are answered. One's life is on the line—figuratively speaking—if one is defeated, the result is death. Contests decide life or death.

However, you must fix your thoughts on emptiness, transcend life and death, and stand resolutely in the void. That is the secret of *budo*.

A graveyard can also be described as a place where old thoughts die. When *misogi* is performed, the spiritual ascends and the material descends. With enough *misogi* over time the spirit is invigorated and returns back to its original purity. A good dojo is the place that facilitates *misogi*. Always keep this in mind.

If you have single-mind concentration throughout your body, it is known as *nen*, and there is no transmigration. In *misogi* one returns to the very beginning. In *budo* training, if you are caught up with selfish thoughts and desires, you will never progress spiritually. *Bu* based on selfish thoughts and desires is a false path. A heart with pure *nen* results in wonderful, compassionate power (*nenpi kannonriki*). Such concentrated mind-power can shatter attacking swords; it is the pure spirit of the gods, the divine energy of emptiness. Use mind-power to fight your battles.

However, mind-power alone cannot defeat another's spirit. You must also capture the actual form of the attack before your eyes and not overlook the present reality. The circle and the triangle work like a rice cake that is kneaded over and over to become solid. Offer your beneficial thoughts to the mirror of the gods. Following the will of the divine to cleanse your thoughts is the principle that should guide you.

The place where the vapor body and liquid body are born is called the hall of *bu*. The graveyard is the place where the spirit and matter separate, but the spirit is purified through *misogi*.

IV

AIKI IS THE MARVELOUS FUNCTIONING OF BREATH

We must unite human and divine nature, bind ourselves to the world, regulate unlimited and temporal energy, and progress along the way of harmony. If you have life in you, you have access to the secrets of the ages, for the truth of the universe resides in each and every human being. The kingdom of heaven is within your real nature.

All things of heaven and earth have breath—the thread of life that ties everything together. The act of breathing connects with all the elements of heaven and earth. You must discover that the individual resonance within our hearts resounds through our senses, our internal organs, and our limbs, tying them together in sequence to link us with the cosmic resonance of existence. The resonance of one's breath, originating from deep within our spirit, animates all things. Breath is the subtle thread that binds us to the universe. This pristine fountain of existence is where our breath and actions originate, and we must utilize it to purify this world of maliciousness.

To gather the universe within your spirit, dwell amid the three worlds of Hidden, Manifest, and Divine. The purpose of Aikido is to harmonize oneself with the divine and work for a better world.

Build a peaceful, beautiful world where there are no wars and no fighting; actualize the great way in heaven and earth. This is the path of Aikido.

Morihei during a demonstration in Hawaii in 1961.

The world is full of accumulated pollution and defilements. That is why the current condition of the world is so bad. However, all this pollution and these defilements can be purged through the principles of Aikido. Aikido reveals to us the true nature of the universe and provides us with the methods for purifying the world through the practice of harmony. This is the original intent of *takemusu aiki*. Advance the cause of world peace in every way possible.

The marvelous functioning of *ki* derives from subtle changes in breath; it is the parent of life. This is the essence of *bu* (love). When you rely on the marvelous function of *ki*, unify mind and body and practice Aikido. Subtle changes in your breath allow you to freely execute techniques. These subtle changes link you to the flow of universal energy.

Subtle changes in breath permeate your being and allow you to move in a free and unhindered manner, under any contingency. When one understands how subtle changes in breath operate, true Aikido techniques are born. Subtle changes in breath are the waves of the void. These waves vary in frequency from concentrated to diffuse. With training, you will be able to respond to them with your entire mind and body.

Techniques must be in tune with universal principles. Techniques that are not in such accord will destroy you. Such techniques are invalid, not the *bu* of *takemusu*. Techniques that are in tune with universal principles bestow the blessings of love. They constitute the *bu* of *takemusu*.

The first step in linking yourself to *takemusu bu* is resonance. The resonance of the body is a spear that strikes the cord of *A UN*, and that generates a tremendous power that fills the universe. The form that this physical resonance assumes is *musubi* [unlimited creativity]. That principle is the fount of creation. It spurs the manifold dimensions of life.

The act of breathing, regardless of whether you are conscious of it or not, naturally ties you to the universe; if you advance in training you can sense your breath spiraling to all corners of the universe. Breathe that universe back inside you. That is the first step in developing breath techniques.

Breathe like this, and your spirit will become truly calm and settled. This is the initial step in developing subtle *aiki* techniques. In time, *aiki* techniques can—indeed must—be performed with no premeditation.

Master the marvelous use of *aiki*, and you will understand the nobility of creation. Breathe spirals up to the right and spirals down to the left. The interaction of water and fire is born, and their friction activates life. The interaction of water and fire is the source of creation and the fount of unlimited power. Understand this, and you will be able to grasp the essence of *aiki*.

Aiki is a cross reaching from heaven to earth, joining breath, yin and yang, and water and fire. Your own breath must blend with this in order to facilitate understanding of the doors of matter and spirit. Physical existence is matter; spirit is the resonance that ties all things together. We must possess the power that propels the universe. Heaven operates according to a design initiated by the opening of the dual doors of spirit and matter. If this did not occur there would be no real human beings. To understand these deep mysteries you must cleanse your heart of impurities.

Morihei performing *misogi-no-jo* in Hawaii during his trip there in 1961.

You must achieve balance between energy, intelligence, virtue, knowledge, and physical activity through *aiki*. How is that achieved? By projecting *ki*. You must comprehend the entire spectrum of *aiki*. The energy of *bu* is an unlimited, irresistible force.

The great god of earth *Kuni no tokotachi* set aright the world through *aiki*. She generated unlimited, ceaseless growth and the world came into being. Everything was accomplished. *Kuni no tokotachi* is a code name for creation and the grand design of universal energy. That name represents the interaction of breath, yin and yang, water and fire. That in turn led to the appearance of *Izanagi* and *Izanami*; through the interaction of *aiki* all things were accomplished.

Takamimusubi and *Kamimusubi* made their hearts round and their bodies triangular in order to progress. When a person secludes himself among steep mountains and hidden valleys, he can link himself to the *ki* of yin and yang. Through *aiki* and mutual integration one can accomplish anything, even the most difficult task. If you practice Aikido meditation (*chinkon-kishin*), you can concentrate your spirit in all aspects of daily life. This is how we investigate the workings of breath. This is the origin of the *U* seed-syllable. With it, you can do anything. I have spent my life training in *bu*, following the lead of the two gods *Izanagi* and *Izanami*; their breath pervades heaven and earth. Breath circulates.

In steep mountains and hidden valleys the power of nature can be sensed. Link the *aiki* of heaven and earth with the *aiki* of your heart. The *aiki* of your spirit and the resonance of your soul will become unified, and you can accomplish great deeds.

In daily training, you must regulate your *ki*. In the practice of Aikido, *ki* naturally functions. *Ki* gives structure to the universe. "In the beginning" means that matter boiled out of molten *ki*. It is not necessary to see this with the naked eye. Your entire body glows with the light of the sun goddess, emitting diamond-like beams that tie everything together. How are we to do this? Utilize the power of compassionate wisdom and true enlightenment.

The universe radiates with auspicious light. Plants, trees, all of nature bursts with spiritual energy; if we human beings can open the stone door

Morihei instructing in Hawaii.

of the soul [and see the light], world peace will arise. The world sparkles with the spiritual energy of our ancestors; the solar system is glowing with marvelous *ki*. Those who understand this are an asset to our world, our country. They work to make *katsuhayabi* a reality. With *misogi* of the world as my guiding principle, when I stand on the Floating Bridge of Heaven, the divine *ki* of *katsuhayabi* descends, and I follow the practice of *takemusu aiki*. This is Aikido, the way established by the divine, the way that provides us with the means to truly perform *misogi*.

Bu eternally strives to elevate matter into spirit; its intent is to harmonize the three worlds. When *Izanagi* and *Izanami* created the world, *misogi* began to operate, and the Floating Bridge of Heaven spanned from corner to corner of the universe. This bridge allows us to accomplish our mission. We follow the example of the god *Susano-o no kami*, who incarnated himself as *Sarutahiko* to provide us guidance in sincerity and love. (He employed the light from the Floating Bridge of Heaven and the descending spiritual energy of *katsuhayabi* to construct a paradise in this world. Do not forget this act.)

This world was manifest as the garden of the gods, the place where they operated and performed their mission, together with human beings. *Susano-o* became lord of this earth; sometimes he was known as the Buddhist deities *Kannon* or *Miroku*. This god wields the *kusanagi* sword [of deep learning and bravery] that unites the *ki* of levels of creation and opens the spirit of myriad things. (When such a bold action is performed, the world is in perfect harmony.) That allows us to protect the three worlds. The gods and goddesses have established this path after great hardship, and as their children we must complete their mission. Heaven and earth will sparkle, and we can hear spiritual sounds everywhere. The days and months will become more and more radiant, the spiritual realm will shine, and we will stand on the Floating Bridge of Heaven. This is Aikido.

Aikido is the source of *bu*. It serves the *kusanagi* sword; it is the divine way of *odo*; it is the flowering of the spirit; its mission is to transform the world. It appears as *Kuki samuhara*. It is the great way of *misogi* that conquers all evil. The *kusanagi* sword reveals the inner principle of existence; it cuts to the heart of things. Let us polish the virtue in our hearts, refine our practice of the great way of *aiki*, and make our minds fresh and pure. Through harmony we can protect and guide the world. This is the spirit of love and nurture for all creation. Our base natures will be elevated. The flower of the spirit will bloom everywhere. The Floating Bridge of Heaven will appear. When this occurs, spiritual discernment—a special spiritual sensitivity—is created. This kind of special sensitivity can spread joy through the world and be a blessing for all people. It allows us to dedicate our lives to serving humankind. Each individual has a role to play, a special talent to perform.

I was enlightened on how to perform the true principles of *aiki* under any circumstances; I vowed to dispel the world's darkness and assist everyone in opening the stone door of his or her spirit, to help everyone realize their noble mission.

In Aikido, one breathes in universal and manifest *ki*, together with the breath of the great earth, blending those energies with his or her own breath to animate existence. This is the marvelous function of *kototama*, as:

Morihei instructing at a seminar in Hawaii.

The exalted techniques of *ki*
calm the soul, and are
vehicles of purification—
guide us with them
O gods of heaven and earth!

From *Tsuki tachi funato no kami* to *Hetsukabe mi kami* there are twelve gods born from *misogi*. The last three were *Amaterasu mi kami* [sun goddess], *Tsukiyomi no o kami* [moon god], and *Susuno-o no kami* [brave god]. These three gods brought the world to completion and established its grand design. The manner in which the world was made and how it operates is a textbook that guides us. That is the spirit we must follow single-mindedly in this world in all our endeavors. That spirit is symbolized by *Susuno-o*. He did slay *Ogetsuhime* [food ogress], but that was an example of a good god killing an evil god to make the world better.

Training (*keiko*) in Aikido is *misogi*. Training is done on the Floating Bridge of Heaven. Training there is a manifestation of the notion that, "In three thousand worlds a single plum flower blossoms."

We have the concept of *sho chiku bai*. The pine is round. It has no front or back. The plum is triangular. Four triangles form a circle. [Four pyramids form a sphere.] This is written in the old texts. The "circle" referred to is our globe, our universe. The four triangles tie everything together and create life. A triangle symbolizes the three creator deities. It is the beginning of science, and it explains how the universe came into being. In response to the divine inspiration, universal breath condensed. In other words, the cosmos appeared. All impurities vanished; the world was elevated.

Aikido is harmony and unity. "In three thousand worlds a single plum flower blossoms" means the dawning of a new era. The form of our body that stands here shows that we have a divine nature, both physical and spiritual. The spiritual side of our nature descends from *Takamimusubi*; the material side descends from *Kuni no tokotachi*. All the deities are descended from and are taught by these primordial gods. Our bodies, our internal organs and limbs, are a creation of the divine. Our sense

Morihei instructing with a smile.

organs, what we can feel and taste, are patterned after the gods *Izanagi* and *Izanami*. You must realize that you are a miniature universe. Your form that stands here is inextricably linked to the entire world. I want all of you to please understand this vital point. Let us be worthy enough to be able to acknowledge and welcome the spirit of life. Welcome it with the teaching of love, not the teaching of an eye for an eye, a tooth for a tooth. It is like drawing an all-encompassing circle. The teaching of love is represented by *Izanagi* and *Izanami*, the unity of breath, yin and yang, water and fire. Human breath circulates inside and outside the body; that is how it functions. The interaction of *Izanagi* and *Izanami* gave birth to the world; this interaction is love.

Bu is all knowledge and all ability; it naturally creates beauty. We have spring, summer, autumn, and winter. The special characteristics of each season arise from subtle changes in nature; those changes are an example of how *bu* works in the world. All of the different kinds of plants and flowers are another example. *Bu* is that which bestows life. That is the purpose of *bu*, its mission.

When one links the void and emptiness and binds oneself to the *A UN ki* of the universe, one's mission in life becomes clear. The energy of the *A UN* breath allows one to board either (or both) the great vehicle or the small vehicle; one can see them in their entirety, from left to right. That kind of energy gave birth to the liberating *bu* spirit and shows us how to appreciate beauty in all its forms. The *A UN* breath operates in both the great and small vehicles circulating left, right, left to dispel evil through *misogi*; this gives birth to *takemusu* in the four and eight directions. This is the symbol of *bu*.

The purifying power of *A UN* breath is a beautiful lotus flower emerging from the world's mire to bloom; this incredible flower can bloom everywhere, opening the flower of the spirit in unthinkable ways. When the flower bears fruit, the mind freely unifies with the body. The union of the spirit and matter is the essence of *bu*. In *misogi* you must not discriminate. You must not oppose the natural order and flow of things. *Bu* is derived from the natural order of the universe.

The first principle in maintaining and guarding the natural order of things is the purification of sin. This is the rationale behind *misogi harae*, a purification rite practiced in our land since ancient times. Sin occurs because of ignorance of the universal, timeless principles of existence and lack of knowledge about the teachings of our ancestors. Such ignorance is the gateway for all wantonness and evil actions.

To purge ourselves of such wantonness and evil actions we need *misogi*. Divest yourself of selfish desires by purifying the sense organs that are leading you astray—the eyes, ears, mouth, whatever they may be. Practice to understand the mind of our ancestors, keep their examples in your heart. Each and every human being is linked to his ancestors by the jewel-like strings of the spirit that are in every living and breathing person.

Since the art of a hand-sword means that the breath of heaven and earth and one's own breath are the same, the movements of the body are similarly based on the yin-yang unity of the hand-sword. If you boldly envelop your opponent with your spirit, you can easily discern his movements, and instantly blend with them right or left—whatever is appropriate. Envelop your opponent with your mind, and you can lead him anywhere you like with your heaven and earth. For example, in response to whatever hand the opponent strikes with, you make the appropriate blending movement to either the left or the right. Transcend the realm of life and death, and even if you receive 99% of an attack and face oblivion directly, you can still clearly see a way out. This kind of attitude is necessary every day when we train.

In the past, military strategy was based on the reality of the battlefield; strategy dictated that you employ the breath of heaven and earth to "flood" the distance between you and the opponent to close the gap—mentally and physically—between oneself and the adversary. If the opponent strikes with fire (yang), you neutralize the attack with water (yin); when the opponent strikes with fire, lead him by becoming like water to swallow and absorb the attack, rendering it harmless. Whenever an opponent strikes, you must use this truth to blend your breath with the attack. Train in this manner, and you well develop wisdom, humanity, and courage. This will give you a true, unshakable spirit, and your entire being will be full of *aiki*. You will enter a state void of all self-importance, a state of "no-self."

Tread this path and move from enlightenment to enlightenment, and you can build a beautiful spirit. The human heart follows the dictates of heaven and earth, so it is vital to train with the ideal of harmonizing heaven/earth, water/fire, yin/yang.

Hands, feet, and hips must be centered and in line, and the mind and body unified. Know that the ability to lead (or be lead by) an attack is determined by the movements of the hands. Lead an attack in order to harmonize with it. You must understand this principle. When your partner wants to pull, the intent to pull arises before the actual action, and that intent is what you must perceive. If you train in this technique, you will be able to fulfill what the opponent lacks; in other words, anticipate any attack and render it harmless with an appropriate response. Aikido is the ability to perceive inadequacies.

The purpose of Aikido is not to down an opponent but to control him spiritually and make him abandon his folly on his own. To make harmony a reality in our world is the spirit that must guide us in our daily training. Every day train to unify mind and body, and refine your spirit.

I aspire to establish true Aikido in this world for the sake of all people. Aikido is all that I am.

Su is the basis of *mi-iki* [sacred breath, cosmic life force]. The universe is *su* in its solidified state. I believe *su* fosters *ki*, knowledge, ethics, and good sense. I call this *odo no kamuzawa*. How do we accomplish this?

It begins on the Floating Bridge of Heaven. When you stand on the Floating Bridge of Heaven, *a* evolves into *me*. *Ame* (heaven) is that which is "self-evolving." The interaction of water and fire is simultaneous: water activates fire, fire activates water. This is the principle that must guide us. That is why I always began my instructions talking about breath.

In order to draw a circle, you must have a firm center. That center is the point from which the circle emerges. Apply that image to acts of love. Love is the primary spirit that stands in the center of this world, tying everything together. One's own breath, one's own spirit derives from that center. Freely breathe in the entire universe.

When it appears there is going to be a conflict, control the fighting before it actually starts. This is the approach of Japanese *budo*. The path of love requires great patience. The path of love is the power and life of this world.

Without *bu*, the nation will perish. *Bu* is the life force that protects love. It is the basis of science.

Arm yourself spiritually and develop an enlightened vision to see through people's falsehoods. If you perfect your spirit, there will no longer be concern for petty things. Love is the most precious object. The solidification of this world is due to the functioning of red and white jewels, but no one in Japan has yet discovered the ramifications of this principle.

The art of politics is to prevent things from festering into problems and to defuse conflicts before they arise.

Aikido is good for the health. It promotes beauty. It teaches good manners and proper deportment. Aikido begins with mutual respect when we sit and bow to one another. We should never act in a rude or improper manner. To train in Aikido is to refine the spirit. It is all about

Morihei performing a purification
ceremony in the Honolulu Dojo.

ki. Fill your senses with *ki*. First of all, perform *chinkon-kishin*. When you start out, unify your spirit. Air (breath) is the key to achieving unity. The human body contains past, present, and future. *Chinkon-kishin* will provide you with the means to understand how the cosmos operates.

In Japan from ancient times we have had traditional methods of meditation and concentration. We incorporate those traditional methods in Aikido training. In the old days, practitioners called their training *iku-musu*. *I* is "expel," *ku* is "inhale," *mu* is "expel," *su* is "inhale." This is the power source of all one's deeds. In ancient times, there was the practice of *torifune* or *furutama*, but we need not rely on such things exclusively today. Make each day anew, advance in a fresh dimension every day. Each and every day investigate something new, always make progress—this is Aikido.

Never become stagnant. Train your body, forge your spirit, and swallow the world in one gulp! Stand boldly, with confidence, wherever you find yourself. Make use of all your innate power and you can accomplish anything. The sword of the spirit and the techniques of *bu* are vehicles to assist us in the reformation of this world.

When we open the door of the spirit, it will give us understanding of all things. Aikido possesses an unlimited power to transform human beings. Our being consists of spirit and matter. In union, the two facets generate *ki* power. Aikido is the power of the spirit. Always train to develop this power; and let us all please train together.

V

LINK YOURSELF TO THE UNIVERSE

Your body is a creation of the universe, housing the spirit; your being is miraculously linked to the essence of the universe—in fact you are one with the universe and that should be the guiding principle of your life. The gift of life that has been bestowed on human beings dictates that they should guard and purify the world. They need to first develop perseverance, and then polish and clarify their thoughts. This will allow them to single-mindedly concentrate on the essential task of unifying mind and body

Unification of mind and body will lead to the development of fundamental techniques. Techniques that are created by *nen* [single-minded concentration, direct perception of the truth] are unlimited in scope. Techniques must reflect universal principles. For this we need true *nen*. Correct and relevant *nen* is essential for the proper practice of *budo*. If you are full of selfish and petty thoughts, you will never make progress in *budo* training. That kind of *budo* is malicious and will result in disaster. *Nen* never focuses on the physical aspects of a confrontation. Link yourself to the cosmos through *kimusubi* [blending of energy]. If *nen* stagnates in the body, life begins to fade. On the other hand, when *nen* is interacting in body and mind, life flourishes. Powerful *nen* can even produce supernatural powers and enlightened insight.

The *nen* that ties your body to the universe will allow you to become

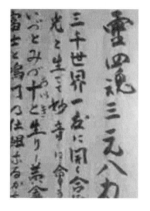

Morihei in Tanabe, Wakayama Prefecture, his birthplace in front of a small Kumano Gongen shrine near his old home.

one with the universe; then you can transcend the realm of life and death and stand at the very center of the cosmos. This is the secret of *budo*.

Nen never contends with the universe. That would shatter its energy. Never think that *nen* is a physical entity that can be detached from the universe. Any thought that contends with the universe will lead to one's destruction. Refine your *nen*, elevate your consciousness, and become one with the universe.

When you link yourself to the marvelous functioning of *ki*, the left side of your body becomes the base of *bu* while the right side receives and ties you to universal energy. When the left begins to blend with the right, one can move in complete freedom.

All the different aspects of the left are the basis of *bu*. When you enter that realm of freedom, your body has a sense of divine lightness. The right derives its power from the left. Use the left as a shield, the right as the source of techniques. This is a principle of nature. Keep this principle in your belly; adapt to any situation by moving without hindrance.

The left is the source of inexhaustible, unlimited *ki*. The right is the vehicle that allows us to link and access ourselves to universal energy. When spiritual discernment activates, the left hand grasps life and death, the right hand controls [stops] it. This is the key to divine techniques.

The beautiful form of this universe, its wonderful mechanisms and inner principles all emanate from one source. Aikido protects and maintains all these inner principles, and nourishes the spirit of love for all things; in the path of Aikido, we stand in the realm of *Masakatsu agatsu katsuhayabi* in order to accomplish our individual missions.

See the universe the way it really is and incorporate that vision in your being. With that vision as your base, enlighten yourself, open your eyes to the truth, and act. You must constantly reflect upon your actions, ceaselessly forge the spirit, and continually advance on the path. That will result in union of mind and body and the development of harmony.

For those who train in *bu*, it is essential to return to the source of existence. For example, look at a flowing mountain stream and ponder its countless variations and transformations.

Like this, in Aikido it is possible to perceive the true nature of the universe from just a partial glimpse of creation. You must train to be able to sense even the most subtle changes in nature.

At present, there is no person I call "master," but I still continue to train. All things in the universe are my teachers and my friends as we serve as fellow guardians of the three worlds of Manifest, Hidden, and Divine. The divine techniques of *Konohanahime* [protector goddess] and the divine will of the gods who reveal perfect harmony are manifest and maintained here.

I take the entire universe as my teacher, all created things as the prod-

Morihei in his fifties.

uct of *bu*. The practice of *bu* summons forth *bu* from within your own being. You must open your own path.

Aikido can reveal the grand design of the universe. It can bring all things to perfection through love. It can harmonize and protect the Manifest, Hidden, and Divine worlds. It can cause the flower of peace to bloom in this world. It can elevate all of humankind. It can lead to spiritual discernment. It can help build a beautiful world. It can spread joy and happiness everywhere. But we who practice Aikido, we who rely on the marvelous qualities of Aikido, must make all these things happen, and strive to turn them into realities.

One's body is a vessel, so you must use spirit and your physical form to manifest the infinitely subtle and marvelous movements of *bu* by continually purifying your six senses. Constantly activate spiritual discernment in your person.

Spiritual discernment allows you to manifest well-centered techniques, techniques that are unimpeded and flexible. Aikido techniques are never rigid or stiff; Aikido techniques are adaptable and free-flowing.

Aikido is based on spiritual discernment, continual growth, and a keen focus on the roots and true forms of the cosmos. Do not forget the universal resonance. See things the way they really are.

In Aikido, it is essential to be enlightened to the principles of heaven, earth, and human beings, and to develop a profound understanding of the great way of the universe and the magnificent, marvelous functioning of *kototama*. Aikido leads the way to world peace and the establishment of heaven on earth. All of us innately possess the divine virtues of purity, beauty, truth, goodness, and love, but we must put them into practice through Aikido. The grand design of the universe is in fact the great way of *bu*. We must follow the example of those past masters of *bu* and not tarnish their memory. They were always probing deeply into the human heart, searching for meaning. Similarly, we should make each day anew, notice how the universe is continually changing, and train daily to create and implement a fresh and vital way of *bu*.

To actually put into practice and achieve universal harmony in this world is not easy, but you most devote your mind and body to the task. With this as your guiding spirit, work to advance world peace.

Aikido is based on the enlightenment I obtained from my training in the arts of the sword, spear, and body; I realized how these arts are derived from universal principles. Aikido is not a method to defeat others, to win battles, or to emerge victorious in war. Victory in Aikido is to complete the appointed task that has been entrusted to you by the universe. Progress in conjunction with the universe. Know the goodness and truthfulness of your path.

When you experience Aikido, it allows you to understand universal principles. When you know yourself, total understanding will come. For

Morihei with his wife Hatsu.

example, in a single movement of a sword, you can absorb an attack completely and become one with the universe. Aikido possesses the sword of the marvelous law. The sword must be wielded for the perfection of the human spirit; a sword used for any other purpose is evil.

What constitutes fundamental human nature? Integrity, faithfulness, respectability, and a compassionate, good, and sincere heart. Truth, goodness, and beauty are our core; we must preserve these virtues. But we must do more than just preserve them—these virtues must be fostered to help us sharpen our senses and become wiser. Above all, there must be sincerity.

Steadfast love creates a sincere heart; use that sincere heart to progress along the way of harmony. To develop a sincere heart you must attain victory over yourself.

The divine form consists of *ichirei shikon-sangen hachiriki*. The divine is one. It fills the universe with life and unlimited splendor. Before there was a heaven, before there was an earth, before there was the universe, there was the great void. Within that void a point appeared. That point is the source of all things. Initially, there was steam, smoke, and mist; brilliant divine energy emerged, creating beams of light that radiated circularly. That point was enveloped by cosmic energy, and the seed-syllable *su* was born. This is the origin of the universe and the spiritual realm. It is the source of nature and breath. According to ancient scriptures, this occurred billions of years ago. As pristine breath expanded, sound emerged. This sound is *kototama*. In the Christian Bible, it says, "In the beginning there was the Word." That "Word" is the seed-syllable *su*. *Su* is the source of all the *kototama*.

This *su* character is not found in the Western world. It only exists in Japan. *Su* vibrated, sending out sound waves up and down, right and left, creating a huge, resonant sphere. This in turn initiated the cosmic breath.

Continual vibration of *su* naturally leads to the birth of the *u*. The *u* functions to separate spirit and matter. This seed-syllable has two dimensions. One ascends upward. That becomes the seed-syllable *a*. The other descends toward earth. That becomes the seed-syllable *o*. The tension between *a* and *o* is the origin of gravity.

Ta ka a ma ha ra is the form of the universe. It is code for the grand design of the cosmos, the concrete expression of divine inspiration of creation. Each family, each individual is a miniature high plain of heaven, a living, breathing manifestation of paradise. In a word, *ta ka a ma ha ra* is the majesty of creation. It represents the foundation of existence. To understand the inner meaning of *ta ka a ma ha ra* and to actualize the divine in real techniques is the purpose of Aikido.

All the different levels of energy come together spiritually to form our path. We breathe in those different levels of energy and harmonize with them, and thus act accordingly, responding to the dictates of those energy patterns. To implement those myriad principles is our mission in Aikido; it is the great path we tread.

To repeat: Aikido illuminates the inner principles of existence and reveals the divine inspiration of creation. The past, present, future, and the entire spectrum of life are within our own bodies. We must clarify, harmonize, and protect the three worlds of Manifest, Hidden, and Divine. That is why we train in Aikido.

Morihei in Kumano.

The universe is initially activated by the seventy-five *kototama*. Each *kototama* has three aspects: *ikumusubi* (generation); *tarumusubi* (expansion); and *tamatsume-taru* (fulfillment).

The eight powers [movement, calm, release, solidification, retraction, extension, unification, division] are the form of *A O U E I*. They embody the heart of the deities' interaction. The tension between the eight powers resulted in a differentiation: lighter, clearer elements rose to heaven; heavier, grosser elements descended to earth. The further interaction between heaven and earth resulted in denser and denser matter that eventually formed the earth. That is the divine work of *tamatsume-taru*. The interaction of the three primal forces of generation—*ikumusubi, tarumusubi, tamatsume-taru*—created the universe.

Aikido is the marvelous functioning of *ki*. The *kototama* are the marvelous functioning of *ichirei shikon-sangen hachiriki*; they animate and operate in everything.

Few people in the world today clearly see the true principles of the universe. The majority of people have no idea how the universe works, on what principles it operates. Such people are not properly integrated with the principles of the universe. They are ignorant of the meaning of life. This results in the disintegration of society and is the source of suffering and upheaval.

Those who wish to remedy this situation and walk along the great path must first unify their own minds and bodies. They must refine the spirit, protect the world, and harmonize heaven and earth. This is the great way of Aikido, its rationale; so do not act contrary to its aims.

The universe changes—for example, there are four seasons of spring, summer, autumn, and winter, and human beings too experience different emotions—joy, anger, sadness, bliss. Each movement is etched with nature's grand design, and we must adapt to and evolve with change. Growth and decay are part of the nature of things, so do not try to deny or oppose the cosmic order.

The mechanism of the universe originates from one source; one source generates the vital power of life through the interaction of heavenly fire and earthly water. The functioning of one's mind and body derives from the one source. This present existence is an expression of the universe's true principles.

If you refine the universal spirit of Aikido and investigate the origin of things, you will be able to understand universal principles and discern the divine mind. Then you will develop a profound love for all things and bring joy to yourself and everyone else living in this world. The day will come when we will be able to greet everyone with a shout and with

Morihei by the ocean in his hometown of Tanabe.

a great and unbridled joy. To spread joy is one reason we practice Aikido. Aikido is the way of harmony with the true principles of the universe. We never assume an attitude opposed to the ways of nature. An attitude that is contrary and contentious will prevent us from following the great way.

Those who link themselves to eternal and immutable principles of the universe through training in *bu* never forget that love is the source of all things; in all aspects of life, cooperative love must be sincerely nourished and encouraged. We in Aikido must follow the natural flow of heaven and strive to actualize the divine mind and divine form.

Those who train in Aikido open the eyes of the heart, hear the divine dictates, and practice sincerely. Attain the great way of *misogi*, practice, move unimpeded through the universe, and refine the spirit. I want all those with open minds to listen to the voice of Aikido. Do not try to reform others. Reform your own mind first. This is the aim of Aikido, it is its message. Each individual has a role to play in spreading this message.

In Ueshiba's Aikido there are no enemies. It is a mistake to consider anyone to be an opponent or enemy, to want to be stronger than anyone else, or to try to defeat anybody. In true *budo*, there are no opponents or enemies. True *budo* is always in tune with the universe; true *budo* always returns to the center of the cosmos. Training in Aikido is not to make one physically powerful, or to make one skillful in combat; it is for the purpose of bringing all the people of the world together in peace, to make things better little by little, to stay centered and in tune with the universe. Aikido is a compass that points us in the right direction so each one of us can fulfill our mission in life. Aikido is the way of harmony. Aikido is the path of love.

My *takemusu aiki* is not derived from religion. Rather, *takemusu aiki* sheds light on the true meaning of religion and helps bring it to perfection.

I am ready for whatever arises; nothing fazes me. I am free of any attachment to the matter of life or death. I leave everything up to the divine. Training is not limited to the time you are holding a sword; in all of your daily actions you must transcend the realm of life and death, and entrust yourself completely to the divine. To repeat:

How beautiful
this form of
heaven and earth
created from the source—
we are members of one family.

The world is full of wonders and is truly beautiful, so let us work together to build heaven on earth. A peaceful world where there is no more war. That is the reason we practice Aikido. Aikido shows us the way.

All of us are part of the universal family. We all originate from the same source. Always keep this truth in mind. Manifest the divine spirit, the divine form, and the divine deportment in your life. To repeat, harmonize spirit and matter to create a balanced world. Do not emphasize one or the other—matter and spirit must be in perfect harmony.

At present, material science is advanced, but spiritual science lags behind. If material and spiritual science can be correctly balanced, an environment will be created that brings out the best in human beings and that will eliminate wars, bringing world peace. If we only practice the physical side of Aikido, it will be impossible to achieve such lofty goals. There is disorder and chaos in the world because people have forgotten we all come from one source. That one source gave birth to matter and spirit and development of scientific laws that drive the universe. The universe is constantly unfolding, bringing new life into being, evolving into fresh forms, and stimulating full development; this is all accomplished through the power of love. All the people of the world are like one family, like one single entity. The past, present, and future are contained in our life. Our task is to breathe in the life force and work to educate others in a positive, pure, and harmonious manner. Those who train in *bu* are always aware of the essential unity of humankind and act sincerely. Fulfill your individual mission on this earth as one member of the universal family.

Look upon the source of the universe as your honorable parents. Do not forget this. Do not forget to be centered there. Being in the center means being surrounded by the outer; if there is an outer, there must be an inner. In other words, elements have an outer and inner dimension that function as a single unit. The source of each individual entity is the divine mind that propels the great spirit of the universe.

Appreciate the beauty manifest in this world and make it your mission in life to spread such beauty everywhere. This is real Aikido.

Stand on the Floating Bridge of Heaven. This makes the single plum flower of three thousand worlds bloom. It creates true *budo*. True *budo* was formed at the beginning of creation. It will endure forever; it is the vital force powering existence.

The present world evolved to what it is today. The universe—material and spiritual—is one cosmic resonance. The universe is like one huge mirror that reflects everything. My duty is to inform you about all these wonderful facets of creation. Although I am acting as a prophet, I realize that I need to become more mature myself, and I strive to make continual progress, little by little, in my understanding of these mysteries.

In response to universal *ki*, nature came into existence. In Shinto cosmology, the various powers of nature are symbolized by deities such as the eight dragon kings, the five male/three female gods, etc.

Aikido is *odo no kamuzawa*. If you are linked to the void and emptiness, the vibrating patterns of the universe will be reflected on your inner mirror. Here is a practical example:

An opponent comes walking toward you; if you are spiritually sensitive to his vibrations, you can read him completely even before you see his form. With good *aiki*, you can instantly sense an opponent's movement and deftly avoid any attack. If an opponent appears right now, you must be ready. There is no room for error. This is *odo no kamuzawa*.

Everything in the world today was made by the divine. Thus, it is the duty of each individual to reform him or herself and to make this world a better place.

Your partner advances holding a wooden sword. Absolutely do not fix your gaze on him. In Aikido, we do not focus on such points as the eyes or the hands. Your mind, not your senses, is the key to evaluation of an attack. This acute awareness of mind is called *nenpi kannonriki* [marvelous redeeming power of compassionate thoughts] in the *Lotus Sutra*.

To understand Aikido, first draw a circle. When a circle is made, it creates a sphere of influence. If you bring an opponent within this sphere of influence, you can throw him with just the touch of a finger. However, it takes a minimum of ten years of serious training to accomplish a feat like this. Let's take a giant leap in our training to make this happen!

Aikido techniques consist of circular, blending movements. Feel the technical movements throughout your body and keep your spirit circular. A circle is completely empty, the emptiness from which all things emerge. Completely empty means perfectly free. From the center of that complete emptiness the universe emerged—this is *ikumusubi* [generating creative force], the parent of all things.

Morihei in front of the Honolulu Aikido Dojo in 1961.

Control the spirit within a circle, and create living techniques. Birth is unlimited. The abundance and fulfillment of life is manifest in a circle. A circle is *kimusubi* and *ikumusubi*. In this world all karmic relationships form a circle; the *bu* of *aiki* is also a circle. Blend matter and spirit; that creates a spiritual center—it is universal *ki*. A circle allows you unlimited possibilities of control.

If there is no spiritual center, there can be no glory, no progress, no harmonization of spirit and matter. To attain an essential spiritual center is to grasp the function of all relationships in the palm of your hand. If you have a soul, that means you are already connected to all other living beings. A circle is unity, freedom, and the source of all techniques.

The birth and manifestation of all the Japanese ways is *takemusu* and the divine activity of the deities of protection. I have a body and technique that give me [and you] the ability to accomplish great things.

Aiki equals humanity and love. Harmonize the nature and technique of the void. *Aiki* will enable you to accomplish your purpose. In Japan, this is called *Masakatsu agatsu*. The sun, moon, and stars do not fight, and they never rest; each fulfills its mission completely. People, full of love, should fit right in with nature.

Aikido appeared to help heal and cleanse the world after World War II. Heretofore there was much fighting and contention, but now we anticipate an era when Japan becomes a kingdom of peace. Fighting and war will destroy our world—instead we must generate the heat and light born from love. To implement this is Aikido. If there is no love everything will disappear. Human beings are created in the divine image.

Now is the chance to learn—teachers and students are shackled by their trifling ideas, so you should study widely and deeply, directly from all the gods, Buddhas, and myriad other deities. This is the spirit of *Masakatsu agatsu katsuhayabi*. It is the responsibility of all of us to make this dream come true.

Let us try seated meditation. In *chinkon-kishin* we can use either *seiza* [formal seated posture] or *chuza* [relaxed posture]. In *seiza* we meditate on the manifest realm for twenty minutes and on the hidden realm for forty minutes. The manifest realm is concerned with outer factors, the physical form of things that were created by *misogi*. In the hidden realm, seek to return to the source of things, to link yourself with true *ki*. All things emanate from *su*, the heart of life and goodness, and you yourself are a *mitama* [individualized spirit] of the divine, containing all wisdom and enlightenment. You should strive to reach your full potential, harness the power of wisdom, and become one with the universe. You will learn how to understand and activate *su*. The method of meditation differs according to the instructor. Cleanse your heart, set aright your *ki*. Act in accordance with nature. This is the essence of *saisei itchi* [belief and actions are one]. If this is not done, the world is cast into darkness; the entire world becomes polluted, as explained in Shinto mythology.

Let us sit in *seiza*. Contemplate your body from the nose to navel. Spread the nostrils, sense how the universe functions—smell, color, the flow of energy. The big toe of the left foot should touch the right. (The left symbolizes *Izanagi* and fire, the right *Izanami* and water. Together they form one body.)

We are the spirit children of those two gods of generation. True *budo* is to illuminate the world of the spirit. Up to now *budo* has only been concerned with the physical world and that is why there has been constant warfare.

Join your fingers in the universal *mudra* [ritual gesture], and close your eyes. Settle your mind and correct your form. Breathe deeply and gather up all the subtle essence of the universe. Inhale the universe and become one with creation. Follow the dictates of nature. You will feel *ki* rise and will experience a sensation of warmth. Your body will fill with spiritual *ki*.

In *kototama* theory we have sounds such as *a, ame, amen,* [*Allah*], expressing the essence of Buddhism, Shinto, Christianity, and Islam. Regarding this there is a long, complicated story of the significance of the red and white jewels in Shinto mythology. Suffice it to say the conjunction of the full tide, heaven, earth, the sun, and the moon created the crystal-clear jewel that we call Aikido.

Heretofore, *budo* was concerned with training in physical forms, but now training in spiritual forms is more important. If you lack a mind set on love, you can never accomplish any great techniques. The stance of love is the stance of *seigan* [triangular posture used in the martial arts]. In Japanese *budo* we don't try to force an opponent to move. *Budo* is based on the principle of non-resistance, a principle of the spiritual world—this is *nenpi kannonriki*. The secret of *bu* is that it has no forms. The heart must be free and *ki* must be fully charged.

All of this was imparted to me by the deity *Sarutahiko* on December 16, 1942, between 2:00 and 3:00 in the morning. All of the gods of Japan gathered and brought *aiki* truly into life, fostering universal spirit and *sho chiku bai* swordsmanship. The double-edged sword of heaven and earth was manifest; that sword symbolizes the spiritual movement that works to purge the world of filth and corruption. To accomplish this, first that terrible war had to end. I was entrusted with a tremendous task: the gods instructed me to construct a thirty-six-mat *aiki jinja* in Iwama. Then the atomic bombs fell on Hiroshima and Nagasaki and the emperor called an end to the war. Since then Japan has been tied together by *aiki*. The true *budo* of the gods will be restored. Within the powerful name of *Ame no murakumo kuki samuhara ryu-o* all the techniques are contained. It is in your blood. As for me, I was an incarnation of the deity *Izunome no mikoto* [the spirit of reformation and renewal].

If you don't put this into practice, nothing will be accomplished. Fortunately, we have gathered together an enthusiastic group of people who train hard. True power resides within the people, namely, *Takehaya susano-o*. The power of the human race is derived from the function of the divine *kusanagi* sword. This is all described in the *Kojiki*. All the gods work together in *aiki*. I am simply one who indicates the way. I do not teach anything. I simply listen to the gods. Use the spirit to active matter. If you get caught up on form you will never be able to fly like lightning and create sparks.

All power is derived from *ki* and is linked to emptiness. Don't shut yourself up in a box. *Ki* brought the physical universe into being, and you must realize this in your soul. Learn about the freedom of *ki*, learn how *ki* flows. Ideally, morning and evening, calm the spirit before the divine for an hour each session. Learn about the all-powerful seed-syllable *su*.

Su expanded into *u* and separated into heaven and earth, yin and yang, water and fire. From *su* everything evolved according to the divine purpose, right up to the present. *A* emerged and the great earth reverberated. *A O U E I* became a divine pillar descending from heaven, creating the *ichirei shikon-sangen hachiriki*. *A* is the emptiness, the nothing that generated everything. It is the source of the fifty seed-syllable sounds. It is nature. *Ame no minaka* is a code for being in the center, the spot of creation. *Aiki* is materialized as circle, triangle, square, and that breath formed the *katakana* syllabary. The essence of the seventy-five sounds is *kototama*. These seed-syllables function unlimitedly and activate the world.

Stand in the outdoor dojo, experience the world as it is described in the *Kojiki*, and enter into the grand design of the universe. Spring, summer, autumn, winter—experience nature in each of its seasonal forms as well. *Ki* is the source of all true strength. Please link yourself to *ki*—that is the first thing that you should do. It is the foundation of your own body and spirit.

Aiki is the functioning of the entire universe from the very beginning.

VI

MISOGI

生

From ancient times, right from the beginning, *aiki* has activated the principles of the universe.

"In the three thousand worlds a single plum flower blossoms."

This is code for how the universe was formed. It symbolizes the interaction of *Izanagi* and *Izanami*. When there was no heaven, suddenly from a single spot creation began. That evolved into Great Space. That spirit of creation can be sensed in the morning sunrise. The holy form of creation is reflected by the rising sun. Everything follows the light of the great sun.

Then, through the interaction of yin and yang, the moon realm appeared. Cosmic breath also emerged as yin and yang, to form a single entity. Like the plum blossom, the spirit is continually renewed year after year. Indeed, it is renewed day after day with the rising sun, glimmering, refreshing each thing. In the beginning there was no heaven, no earth, no world, just the great expanse of *ki* and the great sun. Similarly, we should find the grand purpose, learn from the gods, and establish a joyful, beautiful world. When that goal of Aikido is reached I will be overjoyed. This is the teaching of *sho chiku bai*. First we have the teaching of the pine. A pine has no front or back. It is not of the manifest realm, nor of the

Morihei displays the essence of *irimi-nage*.

hidden realm—it is your body just as it is formed by *musubi*. Learn from the gods and accomplish your mission in life.

What does this mean exactly? There have always been sages in our world. They all revered the sun, especially the sun of a spring morning. They felt sacred *ki* everywhere—in the earth, nature, the mountains, rivers, grasses, and trees. The mountains, the rivers, and the ocean are full of the sacred *ki*. In our country people have always been linked to the sun. We should always be mindful of the great blessings of heaven and earth. Make the world afresh, create each day anew. This is the esteemed purpose of creation with which we must cooperate. It is our duty to work for the benefit of others in our Aikido.

When *Izanagi* and *Izanami* created the physical universe, *Izanami* gave birth to the fire god and had to return to the country of the yellow springs. The country of the yellow springs means the land of pollution. *Izanagi* descended to that land but become terribly polluted and could not return to heaven. To rid himself of such pollution he went to a place called *Yomotsu Hirasaka* [Flat Hill of Hell] and hurled three peaches to drive away the evil spirits chasing him.

In Shinto mythology, peaches are powerful weapons and protection against evil spirits. They are called *Ookamuzumi no kami* [fruit of the gods]. That spirit looks after our world and fosters bravery. There are other acts described in the *Kojiki* regarding rocks, barriers, staffs, pillars, rivers, and places, but in essence they all mean "be sincere and practice *misogi*."

What was above came down and what was below came up. We misinterpret the entire world because of the pollution in our hearts. The earth must be cleansed. If it is not, fighting will continue.

It is our sacred trust to improve our *budo*. We are in god's heart, and we must act divinely. Heretofore, *budo* has had many good points, but we must make it better and better. Right now we are at the level of *misogi* mentioned in the *Kojiki*, describing the beginning of the *budo* we have received. This is the true *budo*.

Misogi occurs on the three levels of Manifest, Hidden, Divine—this world, the hidden realm (Buddhism), and the divine realm (Shinto)—and sets things right.

You must completely reform yourself from top to bottom. Now is the time for the teaching of the pine, the time for reformation of the three worlds.

Aiki is *odo no kamuzawa*. *Misogi* equals *budo*. We must create sincerity. Purify yourself, purify the world. Our work is like a lotus rising from the mire. The union of matter and spirit is the essence of *budo*. *Misogi* must be free of duplicity and not oppose the natural order of things. In order to protect nature we must cleanse ourselves of defilements. We must not be willful and selfish. If we do not understand the teachings of the ancestors, we will create sin. Practice the divine will and do not forget the precious treasures within our body.

Aikido is the way of fostering true human beings, giving birth to good citizens, creating wise people. Our divine parents are *Izanagi* and *Izanami*, so work in their spirit to reform the world and create good. Our *misogi* is to establish peace, brotherhood, and harmony everywhere. Always strive for this. All the myriad gods of the three worlds are really deep within you.

Aiki is peace and harmony, the pine and plum together, the teaching of *sho chiku bai*. It has existed since ancient times. It is a divine teaching fostering true people. It is life.

From the Floating Bridge of Heaven the seed-syllable *a* leads to *me* [*ame*, heaven]. The two join with water and fire and make the manifest and hidden realms. *A o u e i* become the bridge and *su u yu mu* form spirit and matter through *aiki*; spirit and matter are the threads that tie the universe together. Listen to the gods and open your own door to truth. The breath of matter and the breath of spirit—these two elements open the door to the truth. When this occurs, the universe becomes our dojo. The entire universe—with its energy wisdom, virtue, and consciousness—has and always will flow from the gods.

Ichirei shikon-sangen hachiriki—this framework exists in each and every religion. For, example in the Pure Land Buddhism of Amida Nyorai we have *Namu amida butsu*, which is the same as *odo no kamuzawa*. Both are forms of *misogi*, the teaching of the universal grand design. We must always use *ki* to refine the spirit. As time passes, pollution and defilements increase, but human beings have the ability to calm the spirit with the help of the gods, especially *Masakatsu agatsu katsuhayabi ame no oshihomi no kami.*

In even the smallest thing water and fire interact; the entire universe is the solidification of water and fire. Through the interaction of water and fire we receive great, vibrant, transforming diamond power. Water and fire were joined, and this gave birth to the yin and yang of *ki*. This is the path of birth and growth. Training (*keiko*) is a vehicle that allows us to stand in the midst of emptiness, to put forth our spirit. In practice we refine and learn from the superstructure of water and fire. *Izanagi* and *Izanami* are the two pillars around which heaven revolves. Unification is of utmost importance. That is the meaning of "plum blossom." You must research this thoroughly.

An exhalation is *ei*, a circle. It is the breath of all the gods, from start to finish. Master this truth and you will be a fine flower that blooms and radiantly bears much fruit in this world.

Penetrate and perceive the colorless, formless character of the great spirit; learn from the gods how to develop true clarity, purity, holiness, beauty, truth, goodness, and great love. For this we have *misogi* techniques and Aikido. The subtle functioning of *kototama* cleanses the world and purifies heaven, earth, and the nations of the world. Aikido is to learn from the gods and follow the inner principles of all things.

Many people are ignorant of the true form of the universe and know nothing of inner principles. They don't understand that they are the children of the gods. But those who do understand the great path of life work to make things better. Make the world better, strive to create heaven on earth, perform *misogi* to protect the three realms, and use *takemusu aiki* to establish the great way of peace. Never despair or become despondent while performing this task.

In each day of human life there is joy and anger, pain and pleasure, a spring, summer, autumn, winter; times when one's chances are good, times when they are bad. There is growth and decay—each moment follows the natural course of things. From one source fire and water interacted to give us the four souls. From one source the essential powers spread spiritual threads—all this is from the true form of our divine parents. Serve the

Activating the principles of yin and yang energy in his movement, Morihei throws his partner in an instant.

god of *bu*, have a heart full of love, and greet each day with a shout of joy. It is our duty to do this as children of the divine.

Takemusu aiki is a great living spiritual power, not the mind that opposes the path established by the great spirit. *Takemusu aiki* is the maturation of the peach fruit, the Great Buddha *stupa* of our land beaming light. All the myriad gods came into being through *aiki*.

My words and teachings are spoken under divine inspiration, so they are difficult to receive and understand clearly. But everyone should try to learn and think about what I say regarding Aikido every day. Refine your spirit, radiate with joy, develop goodness, advance along the way, become *Izunome*, make yourself one with nature, and accomplish your purpose. Keep the mirror free of defilement and let it radiate light. We in *budo* have been entrusted with a great mission: to establish a holy and peaceful world.

Izanagi represents the physical aspect of the earth, while *Izanami* represents the spiritual element. Now is the time to think of the physical and spiritual as one. Deep inside the physical there is the spiritual. The power of the spirit is activated and polished through *misogi*. If there is no *misogi*, a good world cannot be constructed.

According to *kototama* theory, *mi-so-gi* is explained like this: *mi* is water, yin, fullness, fruit, path, and jewel; *so* is wind, covering, that which is enveloped; *gi* is lively and penetrating, whiteness, bleaching, removal. In short, *misogi* is a cleansing of all defilements, a removal of all obstacles, a radiant state of unadorned purity, the accomplishment of all things, a vibrant state of divine virtue, a spotless universe.

The purpose of Aikido is to implement *misogi*. *Misogi* is *aiki*, *aiki* began with *misogi*. *Bu* keeps the grand design from collapsing. *Aiki* is to be joined with the receptive spirit of the universe.

> In the land of
> finest weapons [brave warriors']
> living souls are linked
> to the spiritual essence of life, and
> bring the divine plan [of reformation and renewal] to fruition

Kami no samuhara is the sword of *Ame no murakumo*. *Ame no murakumo* is universal energy, the spirit of creation, the *A UN* breath of the cosmos. From ancient times it has been a symbol of the divine sword that activates the world.

When I train, the place where I am standing is in the center of heaven and earth. The first step I take with my left foot ties me with all my physical and spiritual ancestors back to the very beginning of creation. I fill myself with the *ki* of *tokotachi*.

The universal grand design is an outpouring of the spirit of creation. This is what we call the Creator. We adhere to the principles of creation. Throws and neutralizing strikes are acts of the gods of *misogi*, they are divine actions; they teach us.

All living things on this earth have something to impart to us. The earth is a great gift to us. Through *aiki* we are linked to all things, and we practice to forge our spirits and realize this truth. The body consists of sense and internal organs. The limbs are *Takamimusubi* and *Kamimusubi*, namely the spiritual and physical threads tying us to our ancestors. Since there are three levels [left, right, center] in the body, *ki* establishes a triangular principle for one's stance. Head movement relies on the movement of both hands. This is to receive the *ki* of the great gods *Izanagi* and *Izanami* and learn from them. The body, limbs, and organs act in accordance to the Creator. The movement of the trunk depends on the movement of the feet. This movement is tied to *Takamimusubi*.

In short, all these gods with different names [representing various principles] instruct and guide us, and we must implement their teachings daily. In regard to this, there is no concept of "we Japanese" and "those foreigners." We are all children of the great gods *Izanagi* and *Izanami*, and we all share the same vital gift of life. The purpose of our life is to learn about this manifest world, the hidden realm, and the realm of the divine. We must link our individual spirit to the universal spirit. This is what I am teaching you, and I ask all of you to study these principles deeply.

Su give birth to the seventy-five seed-syllables that have maintained and sustained existence for billions of years. It is the essence of life. Each and every day we should stand in the dojo and train earnestly, letting *bu* energy circulate right and left; use your left and right feet to tread through heaven and earth. This is *odo no kamuzawa*. Without *misogi* nothing good can be accomplished, nothing beautiful can be created.

Aiki is the great way of *bu*. Many have spoken of this great way, but in fact it all begins [and ends] with *misogi*. In order to walk this path you must perform *misogi*. If you are obstructed spiritually, your soul is damaged, and you cannot act freely. If you are in the midst of pollution and filth, you need purification. In the realm of nature, typhoons and fires are a kind of *misogi*. This is actually a severe but necessary purging. When people perform *misogi* and become receptive to the meaning of the red jewels and white jewels, the gods will instruct them.

The breath of heaven and the breath of earth created yin and yang according to the esteemed will, leading to the creation of human beings. Human beings receive the essence of the universe, the breath of heaven and earth, and the ebb and flow of the tides. Receive both the breath of heaven and the breath of earth and make them one with your own breath. Set aright the spiritual and material aspects of your nature. Realize that each human being has received and contains the entire universe within. It is our duty to protect the world, not to oppose the natural order of things, and to unify the material and the spiritual. Harmonize the different levels of *ki* and become a pillar of integrity in this world. Follow the flow of *aiki*, embrace these teachings, and put them into practice.

Purify your heart on your own and do not depend on others to do this. Use the sword of the spirit to cut through what binds you. This is the great *misogi* taught by the gods. Become a bridge for this world; open the stone door again. To polish the spirit is to open the stone door a second time. Do this and you can change the world. Make everything better.

Heretofore, everything has been measured in terms of material value. The world has been ruled by materialism, and that is the reason there has been constant strife. One should use the material to elevate the spiritual. Spiritual power can set you aright and bring the divine to the surface. This is the essence of *saisei itchi* [religion and daily life as one].

Aikido is *misogi*. It is the vehicle for setting the world aright according to the divine. Material strength is physical power. The famous warriors of

Various movements of the *jo*.

the past were all strong people [but were more than just physically powerful]. However, in today's world, war must cease. Leave off all fighting, return to the divine. *Bu* is the love that fosters life. Aikido must become the true *budo*. Aikido is not a martial art for competing in contests. Those who practice Aikido strive to open the eyes of the heart and practice true sincerity. In Aikido we want to practice to realize *misogi*. We do not want to be stagnant; we want to move freely. We want to eagerly refine the spirit. Those who have heart will listen to the voice of *aiki*. They do not try to reform others. They first of all reform themselves. This is Aikido. This is our message. It is our individual duty.

In order to perform divine techniques, we need *misogi* of both body and spirit. We need to remake the spirit. *Ame no uki hashi*, the Floating Bridge of Heaven, is explained in *kototama* theory like this:

A = self
me = revolve
u = vertical
ki = energy
ha = horizontal
shi = integration of the horizontal and vertical

This naturally gives birth to divine techniques in both the vertical and horizontal dimensions. *Ki* propels our knowledge, virtue, and consciousness. *Ki* permeates our senses. *Ki* is supreme. *Ki* links us physically to all the gods. Aikido elucidates the inner workings of the world. Aikido is based on divine principles. The forging of *ki* is symbolized by the great god *Susano-o*. That deity is the king of strength, the king of *budo*.

Ame no murakumo kuki samuhara ryu-o okami

Ame no murakumo = universal energy and breath.

kuki = the energy that gives birth to creation, the interaction of *Izanagi* and *Izanami*.

samuhara = set aright, rectify, the proper utilization; the interaction of the sun, moon, stars, and the human body. When things are

Morihei using the *jo* to express the divine essence of Aikido movements.

discordant, malicious energy is created and various disasters result. *Samuhara*, through the vehicle of *misogi harai*, is then necessary. It has always been like this in Japan.

ryu-o okami = the guardian deity of Aikido.

Human beings are an essential part of the grand design of creation, but when they forget that truth disaster results. Troubles begin when people are ignorant of universal principles and forget the blessings of nature, and this creates adversity. The practice of *misogi* was initiated to remedy this wantonness. In Aikido we have divine techniques that can set aright the world. Those who practice Aikido must especially learn about *misogi*. Please forge your spirit through daily training. Together with all of you I want to advance the cause of peace everywhere in the world.

The myriad gods and all the wonders they can perform are in fact within each one of us. The divine animates us. We are the universe. *Izanagi* and *Izanami* are eternally interacting inside our bodies. We are an integral element of creation. The spirit animating the *Kojiki* is in our hearts. To practice Aikido is to stand on the Floating Bridge of Heaven; in the practice of Aikido we can perceive reality. It allows us to perform all manner of techniques. We become like *Izanagi* and *Izanami*, bringing all things into being.

You must know your center. Know that your center is in the middle of space. Draw yourself, draw yourself as a circle. A circle has the power to give birth to all things, it revolves and revolves. In advanced martial arts we are taught never to focus on the opponent. To focus on an opponent is to be immediately defeated. Always form a circle that creates life.

Budo so far has focused on the physical, ignoring the divine way and chasing after material things. That is the reason there has been continual strife. Illuminate the world that cannot be seen, the world of the spirit. Pacification of this world is the perfection of true *budo*. Previously, *budo* has only been concerned with forms and patterns, but we should forget all that and rely on the spirit. Without a loving heart, it is difficult to accomplish anything great. The attitude of love is the stance of *seigan* [that allows one to see the formless truth]. In Japanese *budo* we do not become beguiled by an opponent. The secret of *budo* is not in forms. Mastery is in freedom of the heart. Technique and *ki* must be one. This is all taught to us by *Sarutahiko* as incarnated as *Ame no murakumo kuki samuhara ryu-o*. His name includes all the techniques of Aikido.

In a vision I heard a voice tell me, "I am now in your blood." I was transformed into the spirit of *Izunome*. *Izunome* is the deity that combines the rough and gentle soul (*izu*) with the intelligent and happy soul (*mizu*), creating a combined spirit called *Izunome*. However, it is more than just a title. I have to earn it with the help of others. I need to work with you all. The power of the people is represented by *Susano-o*. His power enables human beings to wield the sword of truth, perform *misogi*, and practice Aikido.

THE DIVINE AND
THE HUMAN

In Aikido we are not fighting or contending to win—we emerge victorious by not fighting. It is the principle of non-resistance. It is to be victorious over oneself, victorious in accomplishing your mission in life. It is training in *Masakatsu agatsu katsuhayabi*, to advance along the universal path. You must practice and practice until you realize your inner goodness, your innate truth.

In Aikido we never attack. An attack proves that one is not confident of victory, that one has already been defeated spiritually.

In Aikido we never force the opponent in an unnatural way. Utilize the uncontrolled power of the attack and turn this violence back to the attacker; let him fall of his own accord. Use the subtle methods of *ki*, body, and mind to guide him. The more violent and uncontrolled an attack, the easier it is to control.

We win by not fighting; this is the essence of Aikido, the great value of *Masakatsu agatsu katsuhayabi*.

In heaven, the gods only know about that place and are usually not concerned with human activities. The purpose of training in Aikido is to link god and man. However, gods and human beings have different natures and capacities, and human beings can never completely transcend their particular environment. However, the spirit of *bu* is a vehicle that can facilitate the joining of heaven and earth and result in creation

Against a live blade, Morihei counters with his fan while emitting a piercing *kiai*.

Explaining the one-step *irimi* principle.

of something beautiful. The method of training is to find the glorious path of unlimited transformation and use the one to strike the many. Train to polish the life-giving *kusanagi* sword, and realize the truth. The mind should be as clear as the vast sky, the deepest ocean, and the highest mountain. Do not shrink before any challenge. Foster and nourish all life, great and small.

Use the spirit to forge the physical body. Use your *ki* to overcome all obstacles that confront you, and never avoid any challenge. Do not try to unnaturally control or restrict your opponent. Let your opponent do what he likes. Aikido is to bind with *ki. Nenpi kannonriki* is the stance of love. Practice the principle of non-resistance; this takes time and effort.

The world is full of wisdom, grace, and enlightenment, but you must train to experience those qualities first hand. Then you will understand the source of things and come to know *aiki*.

All things in heaven and earth are members of one family, one body. The past, present, and future are all contained in our breath. Each generation, each era, each year, each day, each family creates its own history, and adds to the accumulated wisdom of the ages. I believe we are all co-evolving and progressing together.

Aiki is the source of *budo* both in Japan and throughout the world. It is the basic principle that reveals the truth of heaven, the truth of earth, the truth of material things. *Budo* is the source of a nation's strength. It is the principle of environmentalism and democracy. Those of us who train in *bu* never forget the spirit of love and protection for all things. We must generate more and more love in this world. Yes, the world is materially advanced, but we need harmony between spiritual and material science in order to overcome the shortcomings of each approach. If we can achieve this, people will stop fighting and the world will be in peace. Do not forget that this is the mission of Aikido. It is not a mere physical martial art. That approach will never get us anywhere. Physical strength is small. In Aikido, we seek to plug into the unlimited power of the universe. In Aikido, each of us can develop a power that is marvelous, bright, and robust.

I ask all of us to train hard. Experience the light and heat and become a sincere human being. The more you train, the more you forge your mind and body. You will surely accomplish great things. Aikido is now practiced all over the world. The light of the Aikido spirit shines everywhere. Create a beautiful paradise wherever you are.

In Aikido training we focus on *ki* development more than on formal patterns. *Ki* development is where the real training lies [*shinken shobu*, "a fight to the finish"]. Originally in the martial arts there were no artificial matches, formal competitions, or referred contests. In a real fight, it is a matter of life or death. To want to defeat an adversary at any cost, by any means, is a great mistake. To murder another human being is the worst sin of all.

In our country, from ancient times it has been believed that on the highest levels there is no killing or destruction in *budo*. In our land, *budo* has always been intended as the great way of peace. It has been for *misogi* of mind and body. To follow the dictates of nature in everyday life and protect others is the key to *bu*. It is a pity that so many people, contentious in nature, did not realize this truth and instead formulated lethal martial arts.

Sometimes my students ask me, "Have you always been undefeated?" I reply, "No, I have experienced failure many times due to inattention and improper attitude. One time I was traveling with my master Sokaku Takeda [1859–1943, Daito Ryu martial artist], running along carrying his baggage, and I nearly collided with an elderly woman who suddenly crossed my path. I just managed to avoid running into her, but from the standpoint of the martial arts that was a defeat, since I was not paying sufficient attention to my surroundings. Another time, I was conducting a class, and while I was demonstrating a basic movement to a fellow named Tetsuomi Hoshi (who had considerable experience in Judo) he suddenly reached out and attempted to throw me. I was able to counter the throw at the last moment, but I had been temporarily caught off guard. I didn't imagine I would be tricked like this, especially not while I was teaching. On another occasion, I was conducting a seminar at a police academy one day when I injured one of the participants who was resisting fiercely. This may have taught him a lesson (not to challenge an instructor), according to the old way of thinking, but I resolved thereafter to refine my technique to allow any partner of mine to escape injury, since no one should get hurt while practicing Aikido. Once I was challenged by a local Sumo wrestler, a big heavy fellow, who was wearing only a loincloth. His body was so sweaty that I couldn't get hold long enough to pin him. I finally got him down and under control; this experience taught me the technique the old-time martial art masters called 'catching a slippery eel.' All of these failures helped me to improve and develop my art."

What do I hope for those of you who are training in Aikido? I want you to observe the way the world works, heed the words of wise people, take the good points you find and make them your own. Open your own door to the truth. Awaken to the true nature of the world: awaken to your own true nature. Realize, reflect, act. Do this continually and you will make steady progress.

Observe a stream as it wends its way through a valley, the water smoothly flowing around the rocks, endlessly transforming itself. The world's wisdom is contained in books, and by studying them we can create new techniques. Observe nature and learn from the true nature of heaven and earth. Realize, reflect, study over and over.

Those who are training in *budo* must realize that the truth of the universe is in their bellies. They must realize how the world moves and learn how to apply new techniques by studying countless books. Do not waste your time away. Make the mountains, rivers, plants, and trees your teachers.

Some people say I am teaching religion, but that is because they are not well informed. I am religious, but I am not teaching a religion, I am telling you how to perfect *budo*. In my study of religion [*Omoto-kyo*], I came across the phrase:

In three thousand worlds a single plum flower blossoms.

and I thought to myself, "Yes, I see. A plum blossom has five petals, symbolizing the five elements—earth, water, fire, wind, and air. The delicate little plum blossom is in fact teaching us about the universe. It reveals the spirit of the universe. "It was my opening of the stone door. I learned from the plum blossom that the universe is complete and perfect in all

Irimi techniques.

three dimensions of Manifest, Hidden, and Divine—everything is just as it is.

Heaven and earth are telling us to live in the present by following the great way, not to long for some future world in the afterlife. Dwell in the eternal here and now, live wholeheartedly in the present reality, be receptive to unlimited existence. The past, present, and future are all contained in the resonance of life. We are in the center of creation, and nowhere else.

When beginners first encounter the brilliance of this gem of a teaching, they have a hard time appreciating it. Their minds are not open and their power is weak. Therefore, in training you must develop a reflective mind and build your spirit. You need to control your passions and foster the *bu* spirit. The way has both spiritual and physical aspects, and you need to unify the two elements. If you practice the inner spiritual art as well as the physical art, you will perceive the clear, bright light of the teaching. The spirit projects beams of light. Physical *bu* emerges from spiritual *bu* and gives substance to the arts of the sword and strategy. Co-evolve, and a beautiful environment can be established on solid scientific principles. Train to make the world peaceful, and the spiritual and physical aspects of *bu* will surely unite.

The past and the future are right here in the present. Try this practice: Face the east, bow with reverence, and shout, "All you great gods please smile upon us!" At such a time, with reverence in your heart, is there anything you want to fight with? Absorb all human beings, every object, in your breath. Paradise will appear before your eyes. The great way lies before you. Do not long for the future. Dwell in the eternal present. All our daily actions are in fact divinely inspired.

Look upon the great act of creation as your parents. Take *ichirei shikon-sangen hachiriki* as the source. In other words, this unlimited universe is the function of one source. We are the heirs to and representatives of countless generations. The universe is within us. *Masakatsu agatsu katsuhayabi* animates our being. Unite with the reality of the universe and co-evolve.

Human beings are an incarnation of *kototama*. Each human being is a pillar of heaven. Take in the subtle essence of the universe in each breath. Stand on the Floating Bridge and act. Follow the way of the gods. Protect and purify the world. The best way to do that is to be peaceful, harmonious, and bright at home, at work, and in society. That is the real test.

Purify your heart by the divine practice of calming the spirit and returning to the source (*chinkon-kishin*). Renew your spirit, activate the *kototama*, create marvelous techniques, and establish a beautiful, radiant world. Make progress, and shine like a jewel. Refine and polish the spirit you have received from your parents for the benefit of all. Make yourself into a living Buddha shrine. Fulfill your mission wherever you find yourself, in any realm. In Japanese religion, this is known as the divine call of *Ushitora no konjin* [the spirit of reform and renewal], the peach fruit of *inui* and *tatsumi* [the zenith and nadir] in the present world.

All the great gifts of heaven—light, heat, power, vibration—are like seeds that sprout, flower, and bear fruit, resulting in a great spiritual harvest. The universe is us; we are the universe. This ideal is the ultimate truth.

Kototama are the cosmic vibrations that propel the universe. We need to shout *kototama* from the Floating Bridge of Heaven. The great god of *bu* instructed us to do so.

Kototama emerged from where the Eight Thunder Gods dwell [a place of fierce energy]. First there were five seed-syllables, and then seven seed-syllables opened to show the way. From the right, *Takamimusubi* appeared, establishing the thirty-one-syllable pattern [of *waka*, Japanese poetry]. This is the origin of *kototama*.

Study sacred scripture deeply, learn the code words, and you will come to comprehend the meaning of Shinto [and other kinds of] mythology. One meaning of *katsuhayabi* is to study sincerely, to discover the great truths, and to shed light on the workings of the world.

Comprehend the principles of heaven and earth, blend the hidden and manifest, make the interaction of water and fire part of your body and mind, and unify heaven, earth, and humankind. Your hands must be linked to universal movements; make your upper and lower body radiate with heat and light, and have no openings. Do not give your opponents any opportunities to overwhelm you. Learn how to harmonize with any attack. In the face of every challenge, remain calm, centered, and optimistic. Keep on the path. Do this, and you can immediately discern any move your opponents make. Guide your opponents to a better way. For example, let your opponent pull any direction he likes—front, back, right, or left. Respond appropriately, left or right, and get behind the attack. Illuminate the realm of life and death. Even if you receive 99% of an opponent's attack there is still a way to escape. Your techniques should be as fast as lightning. Always keep these things in mind when you train, and you will be able to avoid any attack your opponent attempts.

In the old-style martial arts, there are the concepts of *sen* [anticipate physically], *sen no sen* [anticipate mentally], and *go no sen* [anticipate spontaneously], but in Aikido do not think of each of them as something different. In fact, in Aikido it does not matter if an opponent is there or not. Just execute the movements you practice in everyday training and all will be well. The way you move creates the technique. Blend with your opponent, move in conjunction with him. Once again, the movements you practice every day will be effective in applying techniques. This is the reason Aikido is so interesting.

Through Aikido, anyone will be able to control an opponent with a single finger. Consider the nature of human strength like this: draw an imaginary circle with your own center as the central point. Within that sphere you can control even the most physically powerful attacker. As long as he is in your sphere, you can render him powerless, even with just one finger, and control the attack. Always keep yourself in the center. If you lose the center, you lose control.

Circular movement is the key. Imagine a cross within a circle. Stand at the central part of the cross, and let your feet revolve. Form a triangular stance with your feet. Keep the front foot centered and revolve on the back foot. Link yourself to the energy of heaven and earth when you move.

In *aiki*, your energy and universal energy must become one. This is something you must do on your own, all the time. *Ki* forms a cross in the center. *Aiki* is the science of heaven, the manifestation of spiritual science.

When you breathe in, heaven and earth, sound and spirit are harmonized in one beat—that is *kototama*, a reverberation that flies through the cosmos. For this to occur, sound, body, and spirit must be united; then real techniques will appear. The aim of training in Aikido is to unite

Ikkyo pin.

Kokyu-nage.

mind and body and to refine and polish the spirit in order to generate a wonderful power. This is the heart of *budo* training.

When your partner wants to pull, that intention arises in his mind, so let him pull where he wants. Through training, however, you will develop the ability to sense where he is going, supply what he lacks, so to speak, and create a technique that takes advantage of his weakness. Perceiving an opening in your opponent's defenses has always been the key to *budo*.

True *budo* is not for destroying an opponent. It is for disarming an attack spiritually by blending with your opponent and making him joyfully give up the aggression. True *budo* is Aikido. We must foster the spirit of harmony in daily training. When your opponent grabs your wrist, lead him with the movement of your feet and down him with your hands. For the sake of training you must execute the technique to the end without any break in concentration or slackness in body. In training, you need to observe and develop comprehension of the principles of human movement and psychology. *Budo* is the teaching of heaven and earth.

For example, let's say you are surrounded by men armed with spears.

Even if they all come at once, single out one attacker. In the old days, warriors mistakenly used pillars or trees as shields to try to escape. In our case we use the mindset of the attackers as a shield, get out of the circle safely with an *irimi-tenkan* [enter and turn] move, and neutralize the attack. No matter how many opponents there are we can employ *irimi-tenkan* to foil the attack.

Practice that movement and those principles in training. When a group of opponents comes at you, think of them as one person. Use one to strike the many. Don't give any openings or be slack in training.

Unify mind and body and start from there with that as your base. That kind of single-minded concentration will allow you to develop unlimited techniques, techniques that must be based on universal principles. You must always maintain a proper mindset. In training, you cannot get caught up in trivial or selfish thoughts. That creates wantonness. Keep your *nen* free-flowing. This is the *nen* we must polish, the *nen* we must activate in body and mind. The universe is in continual growth, a growth that never stops. That is the spirit we must maintain and know as our source of being. If you do not realize these truths you cannot practice Aikido. Aikido is based on the universal principles of nature, and if you go against them, you will end up destroying yourself. *Nen* does not get caught up on the forms before your eyes. It links itself to the energy of the cosmos. Keep your senses sharp and in tune with the three worlds.

Your body incarnates the grand design of creation. When you breathe, you are breathing in the cosmos, you and the universe are the same. The secret of *budo* is to link your *nen* to universal *ki*, to transcend the realm of life and death, and to stand in the center of the universe. Then genuine techniques will appear, the techniques of love. This is *takemusu aiki*. Tie yourself to that principle and it will resound through your being. This is the breath of *A* and *U*. It is unlimited transformation. Right from the start make this philosophy the base of your techniques.

The universe is one huge reverberation, and we should be in continual communication with that power source. That allows us to perform countless techniques. This is the marvelous functioning of *ki*. Your body and the universe are striking the same cord. This generates light, warmth, and power. When we train in Aikido we should similarly ride the waves of sound and generate light, heat, and power. *Nen* never operates contrary to the universe. It is derived from *ki*, which is very flexible. Never allow your *nen* to separate from the universe.

Do not attempt to consciously refine your *nen*—let it naturally develop through regular mind and body training. Train like this and your techniques will reflect universal principles. The techniques will continually develop in various ways. Stand in the center of the universe, gather up the cosmos inside your belly, and make *Masakatsu agatsu katsuhayabi* a reality:

—Your mind should be in harmony with the functioning of the universe.

—Your body should be in tune with the movement of the universe.

—Body and mind should be one with *ki*, unified with the activity of the universe.

These three principles must be practiced in unison. These three types of forging will help you understand true universal principles, help make your mind bright and clear, and keep your body healthy. In a broader sense, apply these principles when dealing with and resolving various social problems, and use them to establish a peaceful environment all over the world.

In the past, many religious leaders and philosophers have said the same thing, but unfortunately few people heard them, and, on the contrary, people began relying on weapons to fight and to defeat other human beings. Rather than insincere words, we need to put into practice the three principles.

Words should express what is actually in the heart, and the way you speak reveals the way you think about the gods. Your thoughts, speech, and actions should be one, with no duplicity.

I have forged my body through the practice of *budo*. When I grasped the essence of *budo* I realized that mind, body, and *ki* must be unified. The movement of the universe and one's own movement must be as one.

Indeed, self and the universe are a unit that should always be in perfect harmony.

If the marvelous functioning of *ki* is imperfectly understood, disorder and chaos arise everywhere. In short, unify mind, body, and *ki*.

Aikido is the way of truth. Training in Aikido is to foster the truth, to create divine techniques. I know a common complaint is that this is "easy to say, hard to do," but still you must try. Aikido is the forging of mind, body, and *ki*; train in Aikido and you will develop true power.

The universe is based on the spirit of harmony. Aikido helps explain that concept. Each day in Aikido training, by following the natural order of things we cast off our old garments and make ourselves anew. We grow, mature, and advance in our practice. In the beginning I was like a blind man, but through training in *budo* my eyes were opened; I learned about the true nature of heaven and earth. I became one with the universe and discovered to how to perceive and be receptive to its movements. This is real training.

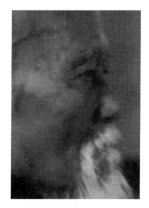

Constant training is the way of Aikido. Think of the world as one true family, one single huge human being, without limits, without end. Be a light in the world. The past, present, and future, countless generations, millions of years, are all within you. Bring the human race to sing together in harmony with one voice. Let us all advance together in fellowship and love. Buddhists say that when this occurs the compassionate light of *Miroku* [savior Buddha of the future] will shine in this world. Human beings are still asleep, and that is why Shinto, Buddhist, and Confucian teachings have appeared in the world to inspire us. We should continue and improve those teachings by constant growth.

Perfect your spirit, be bright and cheerful, act purely, and become united with nature. That is our mission in life. Do not defile the bright mirror of your spirit. Rather be a mirror that reflects the truth, points out the right direction, acts as a mirror of peace.

Sometimes, however, the voice of peace can resound like thunder to shake people awake from their slumber, to turn night into day. *Su* is the eternal sound that energizes your soul and guides your actions. Each of us must fulfill our respective mission. You may, for instance, develop supernatural powers, but if you do not act on what you say, those qualities will be meaningless. We must make world peace happen. Renew, grow, advance, and never stop polishing your spirit. Aikido can enlighten you, reveal to you the glories of heaven and earth, teach you the secrets of the Manifest, Hidden, and Divine realms, and unite you to the universe.

The truth of the universe is manifest in the techniques:

> Heaven, earth, and humankind
> brought together and
> protected by Aikido—
> throughout the vast sea [of existence]
> a great sound of joy.

If you can understand the "great sound of joy," your study of Aikido is complete. Our illustrious predecessors have given us guidance, but it is up to each individual to open his or her way. Christianity and all the great religions of the world are based on love. All the different beliefs and practices are based on a single truth—Love.

Aikido is without limits. I am now seventy-six years old but I continue to train. Our dojo is all of heaven and earth. The way of practice has no borders, has no end. Training is a lifelong practice. It is unlimited. Trust in Aikido. Dwell in Aikido. Cherish heaven and earth. Love all things. This is our mission, the goal of training in Aikido.

Various movements of the sword and *jo* directly transmitted to the previous Doshu Kisshomaru.

VIII

DOKA

道歌

武術とは
神の御姿
御心ぞ
いづとみづとの
御親尊し

Bujutsu towa
kami no misugata
mikokoro zo
izu to mizu tono
mioya toutoshi

The art of bu
is the form of the gods
and their divine heart;
it generates the precious
izu [yang] and mizu [yin].

たたへても
たたへ<ruby>盡<rt>つき</rt></ruby>せぬ
<ruby>合気法<rt>あい き のり</rt></ruby>
<ruby>七十五<rt>なな そ いつ</rt></ruby>つの
<ruby>結<rt>む</rt></ruby>ひ

Tataete mo
tatae tsuki senu
aiki nori
nanaso itsutsu no
muhi

Inexhaustible
the law of aiki
linked to the 75 [kototama]
and the glory
of divine techniques.

（光栄）神業日地月
十になりしの
黄金橋
ひかりうき立て
山彦の中

[Kōei] Kanwaza nitchigetsu
tō ni narishi no
kogane bashi
hikari ukitate
yamabiko no naka

Sun, earth, moon
harmonized perfectly;
the golden bridge sparkles
and floats amid the
mountain echo!

上段は
吾も上段このままに
打ち突く槍を
くつして勝つべし

Jōdan wa
ware mo jōdan kono mama ni
uchitsuku yari o
kusshite katsu beshi

When the opponent assumes jodan,
I too become jodan,
and calmly slash through
the cuts and thrusts of the weapons
to attain victory.

敵下段
同じ構への中段に
上り下りに
移りかむるな

Teki gedan
onaji kamae no chūdan ni
nobori sagari ni
utsuri kamuru na

When the opponent assumes gedan
remain centered in chudan;
do not move
up and down.

日々の
わざの稽古に心せよ
一を以つて
万に当るぞ
武夫の道

Nichinichi no
waza no keiko ni kokoro seyo
ichi o motte
yorozu ni ataru zo
masurao no michi

Day after day
train in the techniques
to foster a mind that uses the one
to strike the many—
this is the way of a warrior.

無明とは
誰やの人か
夕月の
いづるも入るも
知る人ぞなし

Mumyō towa
tareya no hitoka
yūzuki no
izuru mo iru mo
shiru hito zo nashi

Illusion or enlightenment?
Who knows for sure?
It is as hazy
as the emerging
and fading moon.

世の初め
降し給ひし
武の使命
国の守りと
君の御声に

Yo no hajime
kudashi tamaishi
bu no shimei
kuni no mamori to
kimi no mikoe ni

At the beginning of the world
bu appeared to
protect our nation;
it is within the exalted voice
of our leader.

呼びさます
一人の敵も
心せよ
多勢の敵は
前後左右に

Yobisamasu
hitori no teki mo
kokoro seyo
tazei no teki wa
zengo sayū ni

Even when called out
by a single foe
remain on guard:
there are always a host of enemies
front and back, left and right.

天かけり
やみを照らして
降りたちぬ
大海原は
よろこびの声

Ama kakeri
yami o terashite
oritachi nu
ōunabara wa
yorokobi no koe

The heavenly light
that dispels darkness
must descend
across the vast seas
with a shout of joy.

天照す
みいず輝く
この中に
八大力王の
雄叫びやせん

Ama terasu
miizu kagayaku
kono naka ni
hachidai rikiō no
otakebi ya sen

The light of heaven
shines with miizu
in its center:
the King of Eight Powers
shouts his battle cry.

大御親
七十五つの
御情動に
世のいとなみは
いや栄えぬる

Ōmioya
nanaso itsutsu no
gojyōdō ni
yono itonami wa
iya sakae nuru

The seventy-five
parent [kototama]
are the threads
and waves
that tie the glorious universe together.

おのころに
気結びなして
中に立つ
心みがけ
山彦の道

Onokoro ni
kimusubi nashite
naka ni tatsu
kokoro migake
yamabiko no michi

Stand in the
middle of creation,
stand in the middle of your own heart,
and follow the
path of the mountain echo.

かんながら
練り上りたる
御剣は
すめよ光れよ
神の恵みに

Kannagara
neri agari taru
mi tsurugi wa
sumeyo hikareyo
kami no megumi ni

Practice the way of the gods
continually by
wielding the sacred sword;
use it to spread clarity, light,
and the blessings of the gods.

すさの男の
玉の剣^{つるぎ}は
世にいでて
東^{あずま}の空に
光り放てり

Susano-o no
tama no tsurugi wa
yo ni idete
azuma no sora ni
hikari hanateri

Susano-o's
jewel sword
appeared in this world
to shine brightly
in the eastern sky.

主^すの至愛
ひびき生れし
大宇宙
御営^{いとな}みぞ
生れ出でたる

Su no shiai
hibiki umareshi
dai uchū
on itonami zo
umare idetaru

The creator's
all-embracing love
is the resonance that
gives birth and sustains
the universe.

たたえても
たたえ尽せぬ
さむはらの
合気の道は
小戸の神技

Tatae temo
tatae tsuki senu
samuhara no
aiki no michi wa
odo no kanwaza

No matter how much we praise it
it cannot be fully explained—
The samuhara path of aiki
[and the establishment of]
odo no kanwaza.

つきさかきより
霊はらふ
伊都能売の
み親かしこし
神のさむはら

Tsuki sakaki yori
hi harau
izunome no
mioya kashikoshi
kami no samuhara

The piercing spirit of
Izunome
dispels evil;
[that deity] is the awesome parent
of the god's samuhara.

つるぎ技
筆や口には
つくされず
言（こと）ぶれせずに
悟り行へ

Tsurugi waza
fude ya kuchi niwa
tsukusarezu
kotobure sezu ni
satori okonae

The techniques of the magnificent sword
can never be encompassed
by what is written or spoken.
Do not rely on words—
attain enlightenment through practice.

天地人
合気になりし
厳（いづ）の道
守らせ給へ
天地（あめつち）の神

Ten chi jin
aiki ni narishi
izu no michi
mamorase tamae
ame tsuchi no kami

Heaven, earth, humans
united in
izu;
protect and guide us
all gods of heaven and earth!

世の仕組
国の御親の
命もて
勝速日立つ
天の浮橋

Yo no shikumi
kuni no mioya no
inochi mote
katsuhayabi tatsu
ame no ukihashi

Follow the universal dictates
of the national spirit
and fulfill your mission
through katsuhayabi
while standing on the Floating Bridge
　　of Heaven.

すの御言
五十鈴の姿
いろはうた
大地の上を
正すさむはら

Su no mikoto
isuzu no sugata
iroha uta
daichi no ue o
tadasu samuhara

From the sacred sound su
fifty vibrations emerged
on earth to establish
the true realm
of samuhara.

あかき血に
仕組む言霊
此妙技
もちろと〇を
出だしてぞ生む

Akaki chi ni
shikumu kototama
kono myōgi
mochiro to maru o
idashite zo umu

Within the red blood
kototama
are formed
and continually create
countless marvelous techniques.

天地は
汝れは合気と
ひびけども
何も知らずに
神の手枕

Ametsuchi wa
nare wa aiki to
hibike domo
nanimo shirazu ni
kami no temakura

When heaven and earth
become one within you
aiki and its resonance
naturally make you
a servant of the gods.

みちたりし
神の栄えの
大宇宙
二度の岩戸は
天の浮橋

Michitari shi
kami no sakae no
dai uchū
nido no iwato wa
ame no ukihashi

[In Aikido]
the Way is perfected
the glory of the gods sparkles,
the stone door is opened a second time
and the Floating Bridge of Heaven
    [appears].

The perfection of *irimi-nage*.

Note on the Translation

All of Morihei Ueshiba's direct students have commented on how baffled they were by the talks of the Founder of Aikido. As the reader will see in this translation, Morihei's lectures are indeed challenging: they contain a heady mixture of the most profound philosophical speculations on the origin and nature of the universe, constant reference to obscure Shinto myths (complicated by Morihei's idiosyncratic interpretation of those myths), mind-boggling lists of various gods and goddesses, presentation of the esoteric science of sound (*kototama*), discussion of the meaning of ritual purification (*misogi*), instruction on meditation techniques (*chinkon-kishin*), comments on world religions, social criticism, hints for the practice of the art of Aikido, words of inspiration, as well as visions, dreams, personal asides, and historical anecdotes—all jumbled together. However, this is part of the charm of Morihei's presentation of Aikido.

All serious students of Aikido must study Morihei's words and make their own interpretation of his marvelous philosophy of the Art of Peace. To facilitate understanding of the talks, I have added minimal explanations in brackets, simplified the references to Shinto mythology somewhat, and edited out much of the repetition. This translation will make much sense if the reader consults *The Essence of Aikido: Spiritual Teachings of Morihei Ueshiba* (compiled by John Stevens, Kodansha International, 1993) and *The Philosophy of Aikido* (by John Stevens, Kodansha International, 2001).

Study, reflect, be inspired, act, and enjoy!

John Stevens

Morihei guiding his pupils through *kimusubi*.